Basic Bible Survey

Part One
Old Testament

HARVESTIME INTERNATIONAL INSTITUTE

This course is part of the **Harvestime International Institute**, a program designed to equip believers for effective spiritual harvest.

The basic theme of the training is to teach what Jesus taught, that which took men who were fishermen, tax collectors, etc., and changed them into reproductive Christians who reached their world with the Gospel in a demonstration of power.

This manual is a single course in one of several modules of curriculum which moves believers from visualizing through deputizing, multiplying, organizing, and mobilizing to achieve the goal of evangelizing.

© Harvestime International Institute
http://www.harvestime.org

TABLE OF CONTENTS

How To Use This Manual 4
Suggestions For Group Study 5
Course Introduction 6
Course Objectives 7

INTRODUCTION TO THE BIBLE

1. Introducing The Bible 8
2. The Books Of The Bible 20
3. Versions Of The Bible 38
4. An Introduction To Outlining 44

THE OLD TESTAMENT

Introduction To The Books Of Law 49

5. Genesis 50
6. Exodus 55
7. Leviticus 62
8. Numbers 67
9. Deuteronomy 72

Introduction To The Books Of History 76

10. Joshua 77
11. Judges 81
12. Ruth 87
13. I and II Samuel 91
14. I and II Kings 96
15. I and II Chronicles 102
16. Ezra 106
17. Nehemiah 110
18. Esther 115

Introduction To The Books Of Poetry 120

19. Job 121
20. Psalms 126
21. Proverbs 132
22. Ecclesiastes 136
23. Song of Solomon 140

Introduction To The Books Of Prophecy 144

24. Isaiah 147
25. Jeremiah 152
26. Lamentations 156
27. Ezekiel 160
28. Daniel 164
29. Hosea 170
30. Joel 175
31. Amos 179
32. Obadiah 183
33. Jonah 187
34. Micah 191
35. Nahum 195
36. Habakkuk 199
37. Zephaniah 203
38. Haggai 207
39. Zechariah 211
40. Malachi 216

Answers To Self-Tests 220

HOW TO USE THIS MANUAL

MANUAL FORMAT

Each lesson consists of:

Objectives: These are the goals you should achieve by studying the chapter. Read them before starting the lesson.

Key Verse: This verse emphasizes the main concept of the chapter. Memorize it.

Chapter Content: Study each section. Use your Bible to look up any references not printed in the manual.

Self-Test: Take this test after you finish studying the chapter. Try to answer the questions without using your Bible or this manual. When you have concluded the Self-Test, check your answers in the answer section provided at the end of the book.

For Further Study: This section will help you continue your study of the Word of God, improve your study skills, and apply what you have learned to your life and ministry.

Final Examination: If you are enrolled in this course for credit, you received a final examination along with this course. Upon conclusion of this course, you should complete this examination and return it for grading as instructed.

ADDITIONAL MATERIALS NEEDED

You will need a King James version of the Bible.

SUGGESTIONS FOR GROUP STUDY

FIRST MEETING

Opening: Open with prayer and introductions. Get acquainted and register the students.

Establish Group Procedures: Determine who will lead the meetings, the time, place, and dates for the sessions.

Praise And Worship: Invite the presence of the Holy Spirit into your training session.

Distribute Manuals To Students: Introduce the manual title, format, and course objectives provided in the first few pages of the manual.

Make The First Assignment: Students will read the chapters assigned and take the Self-Tests prior to the next meeting. The number of chapters you cover per meeting will depend on chapter length, content, and the abilities of your group.

SECOND AND FOLLOWING MEETINGS

Opening: Pray. Welcome and register any new students and give them a manual. Take attendance. Have a time of praise and worship.

Review: Present a brief summary of what you studied at the last meeting.

Lesson: Discuss each section of the chapter using the **HEADINGS IN CAPITAL BOLD FACED LETTERS** as a teaching outline. Ask students for questions or comments on what they have studied. Apply the lesson to the lives and ministries of your students.

Self-Test: Review the Self-Tests students have completed. (Note: If you do not want the students to have access to the answers to the Self-Tests, you may remove the answer pages from the back of each manual.)

For Further Study: You may do these projects on a group or individual basis.

Final Examination: If your group is enrolled in this course for credit, you received a final examination with this course. Reproduce a copy for each student and administer the exam upon conclusion of this course.

Module: Deputizing
Course: Basic Bible Survey I

COURSE INTRODUCTION

The many references to the Old Testament by Jesus during His earthly ministry illustrate the importance He placed on knowing the content of the Scriptures. Because Jesus stressed the importance of God's Word to the men He trained, Harvestime International Institute presents "*Basic Bible Survey*" as part of its training program to equip men and women to reach their nations with God's message.

"*Basic Bible Survey*" introduces the Bible and discusses its translations and various versions. It presents an overview of Biblical history, geography, and life in Bible times. The course provides an outline for each book of the Bible and teaches outlining skills for expanding these basic outlines into more detailed studies of God's Word.

Information presented on each Bible book includes the author, the people to whom the book was written, the purpose of the book, the key verse, a list of main characters, and an outline of the content. A life and ministry principle is also stated for each book. These principles are basic truths vital to Christian maturity and ministry which you should seek to incorporate into your own life. Helpful charts, maps, and time lines summarizing important facts in condensed form are also included in this course.

The course is divided into two parts:

Part One: Provides introductory material on the Bible and outlines for the books of the Old Testament.

Part Two: Provides outlines for the books of the New Testament.

"*Basic Bible Survey*" is a companion course of "*Creative Bible Study Methods*" which teaches various ways to study the Bible. Both courses are designed to enrich your personal study of God's Word.*

---

* Since each Harvestime International Institute course is designed to be complete in itself, it was necessary to repeat some introductory material from "*Creative Bible Study Methods*." Three of the introductory chapters are similar in both courses.

COURSE OBJECTIVES

Upon completion of this course you will be able to:

- Identify basic divisions of the Bible.

- Explain the difference between versions, translations, and paraphrased editions of the Bible.

- Describe everyday life in Bible times.

- Summarize the chronology of the Bible.

- Create and expand outlines.

- For each book in the Bible state the following:
    - Author
    - To whom the book was written
    - When it was written
    - Purpose of the book
    - Key Verse
    - Life and Ministry Principle

- Continue with a more detailed study of God's Word upon completion of this course.

PART ONE: INTRODUCTION TO THE BIBLE

CHAPTER ONE

INTRODUCING THE BIBLE

OBJECTIVES:

Upon completion of this chapter you will be able to:

- Write the Key Verse from memory.
- Define the word "Bible."
- Define the word "Scripture."
- Explain the origin of the Bible.
- Identify the major purposes of the Bible.
- Identify the Old and New Testaments as the two major divisions of the Bible.
- Name the four divisions of Old Testament books.
- Name the four divisions of New Testament books.
- Explain what is meant by the "unity and diversity" of the Bible.
- Identify the person upon whom the revelation of both testaments center.

KEY VERSES:

> **All Scripture is given by inspiration of God, and is profitable for doctrine, for reproof, for correction, for instruction in righteousness:**
>
> **That the man of God may be perfect, thoroughly furnished unto all good works. (II Timothy 3:16-17)**

INTRODUCTION

This chapter introduces the Bible which is the written Word of the one true God. The word "Bible" means "the books." The Bible is one volume which consists of 66 separate books.

The word "Scripture" is also used to refer to God's Word. This word comes from a Latin word which means "writing." When the word "Scripture" is used with a capital "S" it means the sacred writings of the one true God. The word "Bible" is not used in the Bible. It is a word selected by men as a title for all of God's Words.

ORIGIN OF THE BIBLE

The Bible is the written Word of God. He inspired the words in the Bible and used approximately 40 different men to write down His words. These men wrote over a period of 1500 years. The perfect agreement of these writers is one proof that they were all guided by a single author. That author was God.

Some of the writers wrote down exactly what God said:

> **Take thee a roll of a book, and write therein all the words that I have spoken unto thee against Israel . . . (Jeremiah 36:2)**

Other writers wrote what they experienced or what God revealed concerning the future:

> **Write the things which thou hast seen, and the things which are, and the things which shall be hereafter. (Revelation 1:19)**

All of the writers wrote under God's inspiration the words of His message for us.

THE PURPOSE OF THE BIBLE

The Bible itself records its main purpose:

> **All Scripture is given by inspiration of God, and is profitable for doctrine, for reproof, for correction, for instruction in righteousness:**
>
> **That the man of God may be perfect thoroughly furnished unto all good works. (II Timothy 3:16-17)**

The Scriptures are to be used to teach doctrine, to reprove and correct from evil, and to teach righteousness. They will help you live right and equip you to work for God.

MAJOR DIVISIONS

The Bible is divided into two major sections called the Old Testament and the New Testament. The word "testament" means covenant. A covenant is an agreement. The Old Testament records God's original covenant or agreement with man. The New Testament records the new covenant made by God through His Son, Jesus Christ.

What was the subject of these two agreements? They both concerned restoring sinful man to right relationship with God. God made a law that sin can only be forgiven through the shedding of blood:

> **. . . without shedding of blood is no remission (forgiveness). (Hebrews 9:22)**

Under God's agreement in the Old Testament, blood sacrifices of animals were made by man to obtain forgiveness for sin. This was a symbol of the blood sacrifice Jesus Christ would provide under the new agreement with God. Through the birth, life, death, and resurrection of Jesus, a final sacrifice for sin was made:

> **But Christ being come an high priest of good things to come, by a greater and more perfect tabernacle, not made with hands, that is to say, not of this building;**
>
> **Neither by the blood of goats and calves, but by His own blood he entered in once into the holy place, having obtained eternal redemption for us.**
>
> **For if the blood of bulls and of goats, and the ashes of an heifer sprinkling the unclean, sanctifieth to the purifying of the flesh:**
>
> **How much more shall the blood of Christ who through the eternal Spirit offered Himself without spot to God, purge your conscience from dead works to serve the living God?**
>
> **And for this cause He is the mediator of the new testament, that by means of death, for the redemption the transgressions that were under the first testament, they which are called might receive the promise of eternal inheritance. (Hebrews 9:11-15)**

Both testaments are the Word of God and we must study both in order to understand God's message. The terms "old" and "new" testaments are used to distinguish between God's agreement with man before and after the death of Jesus Christ. We do not disregard the Old Testament simply because it is called "old."

FURTHER DIVISIONS

The Bible is further divided into 66 books. The Old Testament has 39 books. The New Testament contains 27 books. Each book is divided into chapters and verses. Although the content of each book is the Word of God, the division into chapters and verses was made by man. to make it easy to locate specific passages. It would be very difficult to find a passage if the books were all one long paragraph.

Here is a simple diagram that shows the basic divisions of the Bible:

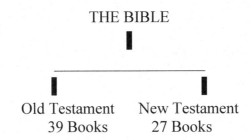

UNITY OF THE BIBLE

When we speak of the unity of the Bible, we mean two things:

ONE: THE BIBLE IS UNITED IN CONTENT:

Even though the Bible was written by many writers over many years, there are no contradictions. One author does not contradict any of the others.

The Bible includes discussion of hundreds of controversial subjects. (A controversial subject is one that creates different opinions when mentioned). Yet the writers of the Bible spoke on such subjects with harmony from the first book of Genesis through the last book of Revelation. This was possible because there was really only one author: God. The writers only recorded the message under His direction and inspiration. For this reason, the content of the Bible is united.

TWO: THE BIBLE IS UNITED IN THEME:

Some people think the Bible is a collection of 66 separate books on different subjects. They do not realize that the Bible is united by a major theme. From beginning to end, the Bible reveals God's special purpose which is summarized in the book of Ephesians:

> **Having made known unto us the mystery of His will, according to His good pleasure which He hath purposed in Himself;**
>
> **That in the dispensation of the fullness of times He might gather together in one all things in Christ, both which are in heaven, and which are on earth; even in Him;**
>
> **In whom also we have obtained an inheritance, being predestinated according to the purpose of Him who worketh all things after the counsel of His own will. (Ephesians 1:9-11)**

The Bible reveals the mystery of God's plan which is the unifying theme of the Bible. It is the revelation of Jesus Christ as the Savior of sinful mankind. Jesus explained how the Old

Testament centered on Him:

> **And He said unto them, These are the words which I spake unto you while I was yet with you, that all things must be fulfilled, which were written in the law of Moses, and in the prophets, and in the psalms concerning me. (Luke 24:44)**

With this introduction, Jesus continued and . . .

> **. . . opened He their understanding that they might understand the scriptures. (Luke 24:45)**

What was the key Jesus gave them to understanding the Scriptures? The fact that its major theme focused on Him:

> **. . . Thus it is written, and thus it behooved Christ to suffer, and to rise from the dead the third day;**
>
> **And that repentance and remission of sins should be preached in His name among all nations, beginning at Jerusalem. And Ye are witnesses of these things. (Luke 24:46-48)**

The Old and New Testaments both tell the story of Jesus. The Old Testament prepares us for its happening and the New Testament tells how it happened. This unites the Bible in one major theme. The people who looked forward to Jesus under the Old Testament were saved from their sins through faith in God's promise. Everyone who looks back to it as having been fulfilled in Jesus Christ is saved in the same way: Through faith that it happened just as God promised.

DIVERSITY OF THE BIBLE

When we speak of the "diversity" of the Bible we mean that the Bible has variety. It records different ways in which God dealt with people and the different ways in which they responded to Him.

The Bible is written in different moods. Some portions express joy while others reflect sorrow. The Bible includes different types of writing. It contains history, poetry, prophecy, letters, adventure, parables, miracles, and love stories. Because of its variety, the Bible has been further divided into major groups of books.

OLD TESTAMENT DIVISIONS

The books of the Old Testament are divided into four major groups: Law, history, poetry and prophecy.

THE BOOKS OF THE LAW:

There are five books of law. The names of these books are:

    Genesis
    Exodus
    Leviticus
    Numbers
    Deuteronomy

These books record the creation of man and the world by God and the early history of man. They tell how God raised up the nation of Israel as a people through which He could reveal Himself to the nations of the world.

These books record the laws of God. The best known parts are the Ten Commandments (Exodus 20:3-17), the greatest of all commandments (Deuteronomy 6:5), and the second greatest commandment (Leviticus 19:18).

Open your Bible and locate the books of Law in the Old Testament. Locate the three verses mentioned in the preceding paragraph and read them. These are an example of the laws of God recorded in these books.

THE BOOKS OF HISTORY:

There are 12 books of history in the Old Testament. The names of the books of history are:

    Joshua
    Judges
    Ruth
    I and II Samuel
    I and II Kings
    I and II Chronicles
    Ezra
    Nehemiah
    Esther

Locate these books in your Bible. They are found right after the books of law. The books of history cover a thousand year history of God's people, Israel. Naturally they do not tell everything that happened, but they record the major events and show the results of both following and ignoring God's law.

THE BOOKS OF POETRY:

There are five books of poetry. The names of the books of poetry are:

- Job
- Psalms
- Proverbs
- Ecclesiastes
- Song of Solomon

These books are the worship books of God's people, Israel. They still are used in worship by believers today. Turn to Psalm 23 and read it. This is an example of the beautiful worship poetry contained in these books.

THE BOOKS OF PROPHECY:

The books of prophecy are the Old Testament are divided into two groups which are called Major and Minor prophetical books. This does not mean the Major Prophets are more important than the Minor Prophets. The title is simply used because the Major Prophets are longer books than the Minor Prophets. There are 17 books of prophecy in the Old Testament. The names of the books of prophecy are:

Major Prophets:

- Isaiah
- Jeremiah
- Lamentations
- Ezekiel
- Daniel

Minor Prophets:

Hosea	Nahum
Joel	Habakkuk
Amos	Zephaniah
Obadiah	Haggai
Jonah	Zechariah
Micah	Malachi

These books are prophetic messages from God to His people about future events. Many of the prophecies have already been fulfilled, but some remain to be fulfilled in the future. Find these prophetic books in your Bible. They are the last books in the Old Testament.

NEW TESTAMENT DIVISIONS

The New Testament has also been divided into four groups: Gospels, History, Letters, and Prophecy.

THE GOSPELS:

There are four books in the Gospels. The names of these books are:

     Matthew   Mark   Luke   John

These books tell about the life, death, and resurrection of Jesus. Their purpose is to lead you to believe that He is the Christ, the Son of God. Find the Gospels in your Bible and then read John 20:31 which states this purpose.

THE BOOK OF HISTORY:

There is one book of history in the New Testament, the book of Acts. This book tells how the church began and fulfilled Christ's commission to spread the Gospel throughout the world. Locate this book in your Bible.

LETTERS:

There are 21 letters in the New Testament. The names of these letters are:

Romans	Titus
I and II Corinthians	Philemon
Galatians	Hebrews
Ephesians	James
Philippians	I and II Peter
Colossians	I, II, and III John
I and II Thessalonians	Jude
I and II Timothy	

The letters are addressed to all believers. Their purpose is to guide them in living and help them do what Jesus commanded. Romans 12 is a good example of their teaching. Turn to this chapter in your Bible and read it. The letters are also sometimes called "epistles" which means letters.

PROPHECY:

Revelation is the only book of prophecy in the New Testament. It tells of the final victory of Jesus and His people. Its purpose is to encourage you to keep living as a Christian should live until the end of time. Its message is summarized in Revelation 2:10.

SELF-TEST

1. Write the Key Verses from memory:

   _____

   _____

   _____

2. What does the word "Bible" mean? _____

3. What does the word "Scripture" mean? _____

4. What are the two major divisions of the Bible?

   _____   _____

5. How many books are there in the Bible? _____

6. Name the four major groups into which Old Testament books are divided:

   _____   _____

   _____   _____

7. Name the four major groups into which New Testament books are divided:

   _____   _____

   _____   _____

8. What is the meaning of the word "testament"?

   _____

   _____

9. What are four main purposes of the Bible? Give a Bible reference to support your answer.

_____

_____

_____

_____

10. What is meant by the "unity of the Bible"?

_____

11. What is meant by the "diversity of the Bible"?

_____

12. Read each statement. If the statement is TRUE put the letter T on the blank in front of it. If the statement is FALSE put the letter F on the blank in front of it:

   a._____ The Bible is the written Word of the one true God.

   b._____ Although God inspired the Bible, He used men to write down His words.

   c._____ Because there were many writers over a period of many years, the Bible contains a lot of contradictions.

   d._____ There is no united theme of the Bible. It is just a collection of books on different subjects.

   e._____ The Major Prophets of the Old Testament are more important than the Minor Prophets.

13. Who is the person on which the revelation of both testaments centers? Give a Bible reference to support your answer._____ Reference_____

(Answers to tests are provided at the conclusion of the final chapter in this manual.)

FOR FURTHER STUDY

The bookmarks on the next page will help you learn the major divisions of the Bible. Cut out the bookmarks on the lines dividing them and place them in your Bible. If you have difficulty in locating the place to insert your bookmarks, use the Table of Contents in the front of your Bible. It lists the books in the order in which they appear in the Bible. It also provides the page number where each book begins.

OLD TESTAMENT

Place bookmark 1 at the beginning of the book of Genesis.

Place bookmark 2 at the beginning of the book of Joshua.

Place bookmark 3 at the beginning of the book of Job.

Place bookmark 4 at the beginning of the book of Isaiah.

NEW TESTAMENT

Place bookmark 5 at the beginning of the book of Matthew.

Place bookmark 6 at the beginning of the book of Acts.

Place bookmark 7 at the beginning of the book of Romans.

Place bookmark 8 at the beginning of the book of Revelation.

You have now located the major divisions of the Bible. Keep using the bookmarks until you can name and locate these divisions by memory.

OLD TESTAMENT LAW (1)	**OLD TESTAMENT HISTORY (2)**	**OLD TESTAMENT POETRY (3)**
GENESIS	JOSHUA	JOB
EXODUS	JUDGES	PSALMS
LEVITICUS	RUTH	PROVERBS
NUMBERS	I SAMUEL	ECCLESIASTES
DEUTERONOMY	II SAMUEL	SONG OF SOLOMON
	I KINGS	
	II KINGS	
	I CHRONICLES	
	II CHRONICLES	
	EZRA	
	NEHEMIAH	
	ESTHER	

OLD TESTAMENT PROPHECY (4)

MAJOR PROPHETS	MINOR PROPHETS:
ISAIAH	HOSEA
JEREMIAH	JOEL
LAMENTATIONS	AMOS
EZEKIEL	OBADIAH
DANIEL	JONAH
	MICAH
	NAHUM
	HABAKKUK
	ZECHARIAH
	HAGGAI
	ZECHARIAH
	MALACHI

NEW TESTAMENT GOSPELS (5)	**NEW TESTAMENT HISTORY (6)**	**NEW TESTAMENT LETTERS (7)**
MATTHEW	ACTS	ROMANS
MARK		I CORINTHIANS
LUKE		II CORINTHIANS
JOHN		GALATIANS
		EPHESIANS
		PHILIPPIANS
		COLOSSIANS
		I THESSALONIANS
		II THESSALONIANS
		I TIMOTHY
		II TIMOTHY
		TITUS
		PHILEMON
		HEBREWS
		JAMES
		I PETER
		II PETER
		I JOHN
		II JOHN
		III JOHN
		JUDE

NEW TESTAMENT PROPHECY (8)

REVELATION

CHAPTER TWO

THE BOOKS OF THE BIBLE

OBJECTIVES:

Upon completion of this chapter you will be able to:

- Write the Key Verse from memory.
- Identify the number of books in the Old Testament.
- Identify the number of books in the New Testament.
- Explain why it is important to have a systematic plan for reading the Bible.
- List four suggestions for successful Bible reading.

KEY VERSE:

Let my cry come near before thee, O Lord; give me understanding according to thy Word. (Psalms 119:169)

INTRODUCTION

In the previous chapter you learned that the Bible is the written Word of God. You learned it is divided into two major sections called the Old Testament and the New Testament. You learned the four divisions of the Old Testament books:

Law
History
Poetry
Prophecy

You also learned the four divisions of the New Testament books:

Gospels
History
Letters
Prophecy

The following chart summarizes what you have learned about the Bible so far:

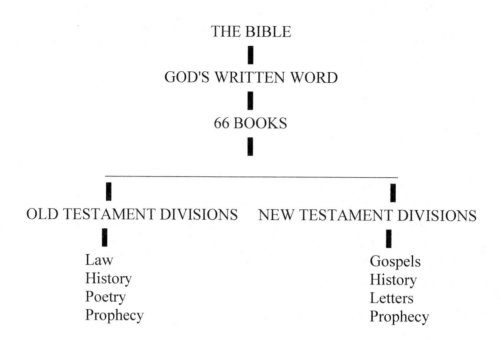

This chapter contains a summary of each of the 66 books of the Bible which make up the major divisions of the Old and New Testaments. It provides an introduction to the content of both testaments. Four suggestions for successful Bible reading are given and you will choose a systematic plan to start reading God's Word.

OLD TESTAMENT BOOKS
(39 Books)

BOOKS OF LAW:

Genesis: Records the beginning of the universe, man, the Sabbath, marriage, sin, sacrifice, nations, and government and key men of God like Abraham, Isaac, Jacob, and Joseph.

Exodus: Details how Israel became a nation with Moses as leader. Israel is delivered from bondage in Egypt and travels to Mt. Sinai where the law of God is given.

Leviticus: This book was a manual of worship for Israel. It provides instruction to the religious leaders and explains how a sinful people can approach a righteous God. It relates to the coming of Jesus Christ as the Lamb of God who takes away the sins of the world.

Numbers: Records Israel's 40 years of wandering in the wilderness which was a result of disobedience to God. The title of the book is from two numberings (population censuses) taken during the long journey.

Deuteronomy: Records the final days of Moses' life and reviews the laws given in Exodus and Leviticus.

BOOKS OF HISTORY:

Joshua: Details how Joshua, the successor of Moses, led the people of Israel into the Promised Land of Canaan. It records the military campaigns and the division of the land among the people.

Judges: Israel turned away from God after Joshua's death. This book records the sad story of their repeated sins and the judges God raised up to deliver them from enemy forces.

Ruth: The story of Ruth, a woman of the Gentile nation of Moab, who chose to serve the God of Israel. She became the great grandmother of David.

I Samuel: This book centers on three persons: Samuel who was the last of the judges of Israel; Saul, the first king of Israel; and David who succeeded Saul as king.

II Samuel: The glorious 40 year reign of King David is recorded in this book.

I Kings: King Solomon's reign and the kings of the divided kingdom through the reigns of Ahab in the north and Jehoshaphat in the south are the subjects of this book.

II Kings: The final decline of Israel and Judah is recalled in this book. God's people fell into deep sin.

I Chronicles: The reign of David and preparations for building the temple are recorded here. The time of this book is the same as II Samuel.

II Chronicles: This book continues Israel's history through Solomon's reign with focus on the southern kingdom. It closes with the decree of Cyrus which permitted the return of the people from Babylon to Jerusalem.

Ezra: The return of the Jews from Babylonian captivity is detailed.

Nehemiah: The rebuilding of Jerusalem's walls under the direction of Nehemiah is recalled by this book. The project was begun about 14 years after Ezra's return with the people.

Esther: God's deliverance of the Jews through Esther and Mordecai is the subject of this book.

BOOKS OF POETRY:

Job: This book is the story of Job, a man who lived around the time of Abraham. The theme is the question of why righteous men suffer.

Psalms: The prayer and praise book of the Bible.

Proverbs: Divine wisdom for practical problems of everyday life.

Ecclesiastes: A discussion of the futility of life apart from God.

Song Of Solomon: The romance of Solomon and his Shulamite bride. The story represents God's love for Israel and of Christ for the church.

BOOKS OF PROPHECY:

Several of these books were written during a period when the nation of Israel was divided into two separate kingdoms: Israel and Judah.

Isaiah: Warns of coming judgment against Judah because of their sin against God.

Jeremiah: Written during the later decline and fall of Judah. Told of the coming judgment and urged surrender to Nebuchadnezzar.

Lamentations: Jeremiah's lament (expression of sorrow) over the destruction of Jerusalem by Babylon.

Ezekiel: Warns first of Jerusalem's impending fall and then foretells its future restoration.

Daniel: The prophet Daniel was captured during the early siege of Judah and taken to Babylon. This book provides historic and prophetic teaching which is important in understanding Bible prophecy.

Hosea: Theme of this book is Israel's unfaithfulness, their punishment, and restoration by God.

Joel: Tells of the plagues which foreshadowed future judgment.

Amos: During a period of material prosperity but moral decay, Amos warned Israel and surrounding nations of God's future judgment on their sin.

Obadiah: God's judgment against Edom, an evil nation located south of the Dead Sea.

Jonah: The story of the prophet Jonah who preached repentance in Ninevah, capitol of the

Assyrian empire. The book reveals God's love and plan of repentance for the Gentiles.

Micah: Another prophecy against Israel's sin. Foretells the birthplace of Jesus 700 years before the event happened.

Nahum: Tells of the impending destruction of Ninevah which had been spared some 150 years earlier through Jonah's preaching.

Habakkuk: Reveals God's plan to punish a sinful nation by an even more sinful one. Teaches that "the just shall live by faith."

Zephaniah: Judgment and restoration of Judah.

Haggai: Urges the Jews to rebuild the temple after a 15 year delay due to enemy resistance.

Zechariah: Further urging to complete the temple and renew spiritual commitment. Foretells Christ's first and second comings.

Malachi: Warns against spiritual shallowness and foretells the coming of John the Baptist and Jesus.

NEW TESTAMENT BOOKS

(27 Books)

THE GOSPELS:

The four books known as the Gospels record the birth, life, ministry, teachings, death and resurrection of Jesus Christ. The approach of each book differs:

Matthew: Emphasizes Jesus Christ as King and was directed especially to the Jews.

Mark: Emphasizes Jesus Christ as the Servant of God and was directed especially to the Romans.

Luke: Presents Jesus Christ as the "Son of Man," the perfect man and Savior of imperfect men.

John: Presents Jesus in His position as the Son of God.

BOOK OF HISTORY:

Acts: The one history book of the New Testament records the early growth of Christianity from the time of Christ's return to Heaven through Paul's imprisonment in Rome. The book covers about 33 years and emphasizes the work of the Holy Spirit.

LETTERS:

Romans: A presentation of the Gospel which stresses salvation by faith alone.

I Corinthians: Written to correct errors of Christian conduct in the local church.

II Corinthians: Speaks of the true ministry of the Gospel, stewardship, and Paul's apostolic authority.

Galatians: Deals with the error of mixing law and faith. The theme is justification by faith alone.

Ephesians: Encourages believers regarding their position in Christ.

Philippians: Emphasizes the joy of Christian unity.

Colossians: Deals with the error of "Gnosticism," a false teachings which denied Jesus was truly Son of God and Son of Man. The book also emphasizes Jesus as head of the Church.

I Thessalonians: Counsel in Christian living and emphasis on the return of Jesus.

II Thessalonians: Further instruction on the Lord's return and how knowledge of this should affect everyday life.

I Timothy: Stresses sound doctrine, orderly church government, and principles to guide the church in the years to come.

II Timothy: Describes the true servant of Jesus Christ. It also warns of the apostasy (spiritual decline) which had already started. It presents the Word of God as the remedy to correct all error.

Titus: Paul's letter to a young minister named Titus who was serving God on the island of Crete. Doctrine and a Godly life are stressed.

Philemon: Paul's intercession for a runaway slave of a wealthy Colossian Christian. It illustrates the intercession of Jesus on the behalf of believers who were once slaves to sin.

Hebrews: Explains the superiority of Christianity over Judaism. Presents Jesus as the Great High Priest and the mediator between God and man.

James: Teaches that true faith is evidenced by works, although salvation is by faith alone.

I Peter: A letter of comfort and encouragement to believers, especially those suffering spiritual attacks from outside the church through unbelievers.

II Peter: A warning against spiritual attacks from within. For example, false teachers who had already "crept" into the Church.

I John: Written to combat Gnosticism which denied Christ's position as Son of God and Son of Man. The book emphasizes fellowship and love among believers and assures true believers of eternal life.

II John: Warns against any compromise with doctrinal error and emphasizes that the truth must be guarded in love.

III John: Warns of the sin of refusing fellowship with those who are true believers.

Jude: Another warning against apostasy and false doctrine. The theme is similar to that of II Peter.

BOOK OF PROPHECY:

Revelation: This prophetic book tells of the final events of world history. It tells of the things which were, are, and which will be in the future plan of God (Revelation 1:19).

SUCCESSFUL BIBLE READING

You will learn much in this course about how to understand and interpret the Bible. You will also learn methods of creative Bible study. But the first step in understanding the Bible is to begin to read it. To help you start reading God's Word we have outlined several different reading plans. These include a plan for those just starting their study as well as a plan for those who are more advanced in the study of God's Word.

First, here are four suggestions for successful Bible reading:

1. **READ DAILY:**

    But his delight is in the law of the Lord; and in His law doth he meditate day and night. (Psalms 1:2)

    God made your physical body so you must have food daily in order to remain healthy. In a similar manner, your spirit must be fed daily with the food of the Word of God if you are to be spiritually healthy:

    . . . It is written, That man shall not live by bread alone, but by every Word of God. (Luke 4:4)

2. READ SELECTIVELY:

Start by reading the "milk" of the word. These are the simple truths of the Word of God:

> **As newborn babes, desire the sincere milk of the Word that ye may grow thereby. (I Peter 2:2)**

Later you will mature spiritually to where you can eat "meat" of the Word of God. This means you will be able to understand more difficult teachings of the Bible:

> **For everyone that useth milk is unskillful in the word of righteousness: for he is a babe.**
>
> **But strong meat belongeth to them that are of full age, even those who by reason of use have their senses exercised to discern both good and evil. (Hebrews 5:13-14)**
>
> **I have fed you with milk, and not with meat; for hitherto ye were not able to bear it . . . (I Corinthians 3:2)**

3. READ PRAYERFULLY:

> **For Ezra had prepared his heart to seek the law of the Lord. (Ezra 7:10)**

Before you start to read, pray to God and ask Him to help you understand the message He has given you through His written Word. Let your prayer be as the Psalmist David prayed:

> **Open thou mine eyes, that I may behold wondrous things out of thy law. (Psalms 119:18)**

4. READ SYSTEMATICALLY:

Some people do not understand God's Word because they do not have a systematic plan for reading. They read a chapter here and there and fail to understand how it all fits together. This is like reading a few pages here and there in a text book on medicine and then trying to set up a medical practice.

The Bible tells us to "search the scriptures" (John 5:39). This means to study them carefully. The Bible is like a text book used in school. You must read it in an orderly way if you are to understand its content. Select one of the following reading schedules and begin reading your Bible daily.

FOR BEGINNERS

If you have never read the Bible before, start with the book of John in the New Testament. This book was written by one of the Disciples of Jesus Christ named John. He tells the story of Jesus in a simple way which is easy to understand. Read one chapter in John each day in the order in which they are found in your Bible. Use the following chart to check off each chapter as you read it.

The Gospel Of John:

____1	____5	____9	____13	____17
____2	____6	____10	____14	____18
____3	____7	____11	____15	____19
____4	____8	____12	____16	____20

THE SHORT SCHEDULE

The short schedule of Bible reading is designed to provide a basic knowledge of the Bible through selected portions of Scripture. Read the selected portions in the order in which they are listed. Use the chart to check off each portion as you complete your reading.

THE NEW TESTAMENT:

____John	____I Thessalonians	____Ephesians
____Mark	____I Corinthians	____II Timothy
____Luke	____Romans	____I Peter
____Acts	____Philemon	____I John
____Romans	____Philippians	____Revelation 1-5; 19:6-22:21

THE OLD TESTAMENT:

____Genesis	____Amos
____Exodus 1-20	____Isaiah 1-12
____Numbers 10:11-21:35	____Jeremiah 1-25;39-33
____Deuteronomy 1-11	____Ruth
____Joshua 1-12; 22-24	____Jonah
____Judges 1-3	____Psalms 1-23
____I Samuel 1-3, 9-10,1 3,15-18,31	____Job 1-14, 38-42
____II Samuel 1	____Proverbs 1-9
____I Kings 1-11	____Daniel 1-6
____Nehemiah	

THE LONGER SCHEDULE

This reading plan covers the Bible in greater depth than the Short Schedule, but it does not cover the entire Bible.

NEW TESTAMENT:

_____ Mark
_____ Matthew
_____ John
_____ Luke
_____ Acts
_____ I Thessalonians
_____ II Thessalonians
_____ I Corinthians
_____ II Corinthians
_____ Galatians
_____ Romans
_____ Philemon
_____ Colossians

_____ Philippians
_____ Ephesians
_____ II Timothy
_____ Titus
_____ I Timothy
_____ I Peter
_____ Hebrews
_____ James
_____ I John
_____ II John
_____ III John
_____ Jude
_____ II Peter
_____ Revelation 1-5 and 19:6-22:21

OLD TESTAMENT:

_____ Genesis
_____ Exodus (1-24)
_____ Leviticus 1-6:7
_____ Numbers 10:11-21:35
_____ Deuteronomy 1-11 and 27-34
_____ Joshua 1-12 and 22-24
_____ Judges 1-16
_____ I Samuel
_____ II Samuel
_____ I Kings
_____ II Kings
_____ I Chronicles
_____ II Chronicles
_____ Ezra
_____ Nehemiah
_____ Amos
_____ Hosea
_____ Micah
_____ Isaiah 1-12
_____ Zephaniah

_____ Jeremiah 1-25 and 30-33
_____ Nahum
_____ Habakkuk
_____ Ezekiel 1-24 and 33-39
_____ Obadiah
_____ Lamentations
_____ Isaiah 40-66
_____ Zechariah 1-8
_____ Malachi
_____ Joel
_____ Ruth
_____ Jonah
_____ Psalms
_____ Job
_____ Proverbs 1-9
_____ Song of Solomon
_____ Ecclesiastes
_____ Esther
_____ Daniel

THE COMPLETE SCHEDULE

The complete Bible reading schedule takes you through the entire Bible in one year.

January

_____ 1. Genesis 1-2
_____ 2. Genesis 3-5
_____ 3. Genesis 6-9
_____ 4. Genesis 10-11
_____ 5. Genesis 12-15
_____ 6. Genesis 16-19
_____ 7. Genesis 20-22
_____ 8. Genesis 23-26
_____ 9. Genesis 27-29
_____ 10. Genesis 30-32
_____ 11. Genesis 33-36
_____ 12. Genesis 37-39
_____ 13. Genesis 40-42
_____ 14. Genesis 43-46
_____ 15. Genesis 47-50
_____ 16. Job 1-4
_____ 17. Job 5-7
_____ 18. Job 8-10
_____ 19. Job 11-13
_____ 20. Job 14-17
_____ 21. Job 18-20
_____ 22. Job 21-24
_____ 23. Job 25-27
_____ 24. Job 28-31
_____ 25. Job 32-34
_____ 26. Job 35-37
_____ 27. Job 38-42
_____ 28. Exodus 1-4
_____ 29. Exodus 5-7
_____ 30. Exodus 8-10
_____ 31. Exodus 11-13

February

_____ 1. Exodus 14-17
_____ 2. Exodus 18-20
_____ 3. Exodus 21-24
_____ 4. Exodus 25-27
_____ 5. Exodus 28-31
_____ 6. Exodus 32-34
_____ 7. Exodus 35-37
_____ 8. Exodus 38-40
_____ 9. Leviticus 1-4
_____ 10. Leviticus 5-7
_____ 11. Leviticus 8-10
_____ 12. Leviticus 11-13
_____ 13. Leviticus 14-16
_____ 14. Leviticus 17-19
_____ 15. Leviticus 20-23
_____ 16. Leviticus 24-27
_____ 17. Numbers 1-3
_____ 18. Numbers 4-6
_____ 19. Numbers 7-10
_____ 20. Numbers 11-14
_____ 21. Numbers 15-17
_____ 22. Numbers 18-20
_____ 23. Numbers 21-24
_____ 24. Numbers 25-27
_____ 25. Numbers 28-30
_____ 26. Numbers 31-33
_____ 27. Numbers 34-36
_____ 28. Deuteronomy 1-3

(The Complete Schedule Continued)

March		April	
____1.	Deuteronomy 4-6	____1.	I Samuel 21-24
____2.	Deuteronomy 7-9	____2.	I Samuel 25-28
____3.	Deuteronomy 10-12	____3.	I Samuel 29-31
____4.	Deuteronomy 13-16	____4.	II Samuel 1-4
____5.	Deuteronomy 17-19	____5.	II Samuel 5-8
____6.	Deuteronomy 20-22	____6.	II Samuel 9-12
____7.	Deuteronomy 23-25	____7.	II Samuel 13-15
____8.	Deuteronomy 26-28	____8.	II Samuel 16-18
____9.	Deuteronomy 29-31	____9.	II Samuel 19-21
____10.	Deuteronomy 32-34	____10.	II Samuel 22-24
____11.	Joshua 1-3	____11.	Psalms 1-3
____12.	Joshua 4-6	____12.	Psalms 4-6
____13.	Joshua 7-9	____13.	Psalms 7-9
____14.	Joshua 10-12	____14.	Psalms 10-12
____15.	Joshua 13-15	____15.	Psalms 13-15
____16.	Joshua 16-18	____16.	Psalms 16-18
____17.	Joshua 19-21	____17.	Psalms 19-21
____18.	Joshua 22-24	____18.	Psalms 22-24
____19.	Judges 1-4	____19.	Psalms 25-27
____20.	Judges 5-8	____20.	Psalms 28-30
____21.	Judges 9-12	____21.	Psalms 31-33
____22.	Judges 13-15	____22.	Psalms 34-36
____23.	Judges 16-18	____23.	Psalms 37-39
____24.	Judges 19-21	____24.	Psalms 40-42
____25.	Ruth 1-4	____25.	Psalms 43-45
____26.	I Samuel 1-3	____26.	Psalms 46-48
____27.	I Samuel 4-7	____27.	Psalms 49-51
____28.	I Samuel 8-10	____28.	Psalms 52-54
____29.	I Samuel 11-13	____29.	Psalms 55-57
____30.	I Samuel 14-16	____30.	Psalms 58-60
____31.	I Samuel 17-20		

(The Complete Schedule Continued)

	May			**June**	
_____	1.	Psalms 61-63	_____	1.	Proverbs 1-3
_____	2.	Psalms 64-66	_____	2.	Proverbs 4-7
_____	3.	Psalms 67-69	_____	3.	Proverbs 8-11
_____	4.	Psalms 70-72	_____	4.	Proverbs 12-14
_____	5.	Psalms 73-75	_____	5.	Proverbs 15-18
_____	6.	Psalms 76-78	_____	6.	Proverbs 19-21
_____	7.	Psalms 79-81	_____	7.	Proverbs 22-24
_____	8.	Psalms 82-84	_____	8.	Proverbs 25-28
_____	9.	Psalms 85-87	_____	9.	Proverbs 29-31
_____	10.	Psalms 88-90	_____	10.	Ecclesiastes 1-3
_____	11.	Psalms 91-93	_____	11.	Ecclesiastes 4-6
_____	12.	Psalms 94-96	_____	12.	Ecclesiastes 7-9
_____	13.	Psalms 97-99	_____	13.	Ecclesiastes 10-12
_____	14.	Psalms 100-102	_____	14.	Songs 1-4
_____	15.	Psalms 103-105	_____	15.	Songs 5-8
_____	16.	Psalms 106-108	_____	16.	I Kings 5-7
_____	17.	Psalms 109-111	_____	17.	I Kings 8-10
_____	18.	Psalms 112-114	_____	18.	I Kings 11-13
_____	19.	Psalms 115-118	_____	19.	I Kings 14-16
_____	20.	Psalms 119	_____	20.	I Kings 17-19
_____	21.	Psalms 120-123	_____	21.	I Kings 20-22
_____	22.	Psalms 124-126	_____	22.	II Kings 1-3
_____	23.	Psalms 127-129	_____	23.	II Kings 4-6
_____	24.	Psalms 130-132	_____	24.	II Kings 7-10
_____	25.	Psalms 133-135	_____	25.	II Kings 11-14:20
_____	26.	Psalms 136-138	_____	26.	Joel 1-3
_____	27.	Psalms 139-141	_____	27.	II Kings 14:21-25; Jonah 1-4
_____	28.	Psalms 142-144	_____	28.	II Kings 14:26-29; Amos 1-3
_____	29.	Psalms 145-147	_____	29.	Amos 4-6
_____	30.	Psalms 148-150	_____	30.	Amos 7-9
_____	31.	I Kings 1-4			

(The Complete Schedule Continued)

July

_____ 1. II Kings 15-17
_____ 2. Hosea 1-4
_____ 3. Hosea 5-7
_____ 4. Hosea 8-10
_____ 5. Hosea 11-14
_____ 6. II Kings 18-19
_____ 7. Isaiah 1-3
_____ 8. Isaiah 4-6
_____ 9. Isaiah 7-9
_____ 10. Isaiah 10-12
_____ 11. Isaiah 13-15
_____ 12. Isaiah 16-18
_____ 13. Isaiah 19-21
_____ 14. Isaiah 22-24
_____ 15. Isaiah 25-27
_____ 16. Isaiah 28-30
_____ 17. Isaiah 31-33
_____ 18. Isaiah 34-36
_____ 19. Isaiah 37-39
_____ 20. Isaiah 40-42
_____ 21. Isaiah 43-45
_____ 22. Isaiah 46-48
_____ 23. Isaiah 49-51
_____ 24. Isaiah 52-54
_____ 25. Isaiah 55-57
_____ 26. Isaiah 58-60
_____ 27. Isaiah 61-63
_____ 28. Isaiah 64-66
_____ 29. Micah 1-4
_____ 30. Micah 5-7
_____ 31. Nahum 1-3

August

_____ 1. II Kings 20-21
_____ 2. Zephaniah 1-3
_____ 3. Habakkuk 1-3
_____ 4. II Kings 22-25
_____ 5. Obadiah/Jeremiah 1-2
_____ 6. Jeremiah 3-5
_____ 7. Jeremiah 6-8
_____ 8. Jeremiah 9-12
_____ 9. Jeremiah 13-16
_____ 10. Jeremiah 17-20
_____ 11. Jeremiah 21-23
_____ 12. Jeremiah 24-26
_____ 13. Jeremiah 27-29
_____ 14. Jeremiah 30-32
_____ 15. Jeremiah 33-36
_____ 16. Jeremiah 37-39
_____ 17. Jeremiah 40-42
_____ 18. Jeremiah 43-46
_____ 19. Jeremiah 47-49
_____ 20. Jeremiah 50-52
_____ 21. Lamentations 1-5
_____ 22. I Chronicles 1-3
_____ 23. I Chronicles 4-6
_____ 24. I Chronicles 7-9
_____ 25. I Chronicles 10-13
_____ 26. I Chronicles 14-16
_____ 27. I Chronicles 17-19
_____ 28. I Chronicles 20-23
_____ 29. I Chronicles 24-26
_____ 30. I Chronicles 27-29
_____ 31. II Chronicles 1-3

(The Complete Schedule Continued)

	September		**October**
___ 1.	II Chronicles 4-6	___ 1.	Esther 4-7
___ 2.	II Chronicles 7-9	___ 2.	Esther 8-10
___ 3.	II Chronicles 10-13	___ 3.	Ezra 1-4
___ 4.	II Chronicles 14-16	___ 4.	Haggai 1-2/Zechariah 1-2
___ 5.	II Chronicles 17-19	___ 5.	Zechariah 1-2
___ 6.	II Chronicles 20-22	___ 6.	Zechariah 3-6
___ 7.	II Chronicles 23-25	___ 7.	Zechariah 7-10
___ 8.	II Chronicles 26-29	___ 8.	Ezra 5-7
___ 9.	II Chronicles 30-32	___ 9.	Ezra 8-10
___ 10.	II Chronicles 33-36	___ 10.	Nehemiah 1-3
___ 11.	Ezekiel 1-3	___ 11.	Nehemiah 4-6
___ 12.	Ezekiel 4-7	___ 12.	Nehemiah 7-9
___ 13.	Ezekiel 8-11	___ 13.	Nehemiah 10-13
___ 14.	Ezekiel 12-14	___ 14.	Malachi 1-4
___ 15.	Ezekiel 15-18	___ 15.	Matthew 1-4
___ 16.	Ezekiel 19-21	___ 16.	Matthew 5-7
___ 17.	Ezekiel 22-24	___ 17.	Matthew 8-11
___ 18.	Ezekiel 25-27	___ 18.	Matthew 12-15
___ 19.	Ezekiel 28-30	___ 19.	Matthew 16-19
___ 20.	Ezekiel 31-33	___ 20.	Matthew 20-22
___ 21.	Ezekiel 34-36	___ 21.	Matthew 23-25
___ 22.	Ezekiel 37-39	___ 22.	Matthew 26-28
___ 23.	Ezekiel 40-42	___ 23.	Mark 1-3
___ 24.	Ezekiel 43-45	___ 24.	Mark 4-6
___ 25.	Ezekiel 46-48	___ 25.	Mark 7-10
___ 26.	Daniel 1-3	___ 26.	Mark 11-13
___ 27.	Daniel 4-6	___ 27.	Mark 14-16
___ 28.	Daniel 7-9	___ 28.	Luke 1-3
___ 29.	Daniel 10-12	___ 29.	Luke 4-6
___ 30.	Esther 1-3	___ 30.	Luke 7-9
		___ 31.	Luke 10-13

(The Complete Schedule Continued)

	November		December
_____1.	Luke 14-17	_____1.	Romans 5-8
_____2.	Luke 18-21	_____2.	Romans 9-11
_____3.	Luke 22-24	_____3.	Romans 12-16
_____4.	John 1-3	_____4.	Acts 20:3-22
_____5.	John 4-6	_____5.	Acts 23-25
_____6.	John 7-10	_____6.	Acts 26-28
_____7.	John 11-13	_____7.	Ephesians 1-3
_____8.	John 14-17	_____8.	Ephesians 4-6
_____9.	John 18-21	_____9.	Philippians 1-4
_____10.	Acts 1-2	_____10.	Colossians 1-4
_____11.	Acts 3-5	_____11.	Hebrews 1-4
_____12.	Acts 6-9	_____12.	Hebrews 5-7
_____13.	Acts 10-12	_____13.	Hebrews 8-10
_____14.	Acts 13-14	_____14.	Hebrews 11-13
_____15.	James 1-2	_____15.	Philemon/I Peter 1-2
_____16.	James 3-5	_____16.	I Peter 3-5
_____17.	Galatians 1-3	_____17.	II Peter 1-3
_____18.	Galatians 4-6	_____18.	I Timothy 1-3
_____19.	Acts 15-18:11	_____19.	I Timothy 4-6
_____20.	I Thessalonians 1-5	_____20.	Titus 1-3
_____21.	II Thessalonians 1-3	_____21.	II Timothy 1-4
_____22.	I Corinthians 1-4	_____22.	I John 1-2; Acts 18:12-19:10
_____23.	I John 3-5	_____23.	I Corinthians 5-8
_____24.	II John, III John	_____24.	I Corinthians 9-12
_____25.	Revelation 1-3, Jude	_____25.	I Corinthians 13-16
_____26.	Revelation 4-6	_____26.	Acts 19:11-20:1; II Corinthians 1-3
_____27.	Revelation 7-9	_____27.	II Corinthians 4-6
_____28.	Revelation 10-12	_____28.	II Corinthians 7-9
_____29.	Revelation 13-15	_____29.	II Corinthians 10-13
_____30.	Revelation 16-18	_____30.	Acts 20:2/Romans 1-4
_____31.	Revelation 19-22		

SELF-TEST

1. Write the Key Verse from memory.

   _____

   _____

   _____

2. How many books are in the Old Testament?

   _____

3. How many books are in the New Testament?

   _____

4. Why is it important to have a systematic plan for reading the Bible?

   _____

   _____

   _____

5. What were the four suggestions for successful Bible reading?

   _____

   _____

   _____

   _____

(Answers to tests are provided at the conclusion of the final chapter in this manual.)

FOR FURTHER STUDY

-Review the descriptions of each book of the Bible given in this chapter.
-Write the name of each book of the Bible below.
-By the name of each book summarize its basic content in three or four words.
-The first two are done as examples for you to follow.
  (By condensing material in this manner you will be able to develop a general knowledge of the content of the entire Bible.)

Name Of Book	Content
Genesis	Book of beginnings
Exodus	Exit from Egypt

CHAPTER THREE

VERSIONS OF THE BIBLE

OBJECTIVES:

Upon completion of this chapter you will be able to:

- Write the Key Verse from memory.
- Name the three languages in which the Bible was written.
- Define the word "version."
- Explain the difference between a translation and a paraphrase version of the Bible.

KEY VERSE:

> **The Lord gave the Word: great was the company of those that published it. (Psalms 68:11)**

INTRODUCTION

This chapter identifies the original languages in which the Bible was written and explains how the Scriptures have been translated into other languages. You will learn the difference between a translation and a paraphrase version of the Bible. Examples from various versions of the Bible are provided.

THREE LANGUAGES

The Bible was originally written in three languages. Most of the Old Testament was written in Hebrew except for parts of the books of Daniel and Nehemiah which were written in Aramaic. The New Testament was written in Greek.

None of the original manuscripts of the Bible are now in existence. Some good manuscripts exist which are copies of the original. Versions are translations of these copies of the original manuscripts. From early times men saw the necessity of translating the Bible so everyone could read it in their own language.

No translation is exact because no two languages are exactly alike. Some words used in the Bible do not even exist in different languages. For example, there is a tribe of Indians in Ecuador, South America, called the Auca Indians. When missionaries first contacted them, these

Indians did not know how to read or write. There were no words in their language for "writing" or "book."

The Auca Indians did have a custom of carving identification marks on their property. Since there were no words in their language for scriptures, writing, or book, when the Bible was translated for them it was called "God's Carving." This identified it as something belonging to God. This is just one example of the difficulties in translating the Bible into various languages.

TRANSLATIONS AND PARAPHRASES

There are many different versions of the Bible. The word "version" means a Bible written in a language different from those in which God's Word was originally written. There are two main types of versions of the Bible: Translations and paraphrases.

TRANSLATION:

A translation is an effort to express what the Greek, Hebrew, and Aramaic words actually say. It gives as nearly as possible a literal word by word translation. Extra words are inserted only when it is necessary in order for the reader to understand the meaning.

PARAPHRASE:

A paraphrase does not attempt to translate word for word. It translates thought by thought. A paraphrase is a restatement of the meaning of a passage. Paraphrase versions are easier to read and understand because they are written in modern vocabulary and grammar, but they are not an exact translation of God's Word.

The "For Further Study" section of this chapter provides examples from several English versions of the Bible for you to compare. These illustrate the differences in translation and paraphrase versions.

SELECTING A STUDY BIBLE

For purposes of this course and Bible study in general, we recommend use of the King James version of the Bible. There are several reasons for this:

FIRST:

The King James Bible is very accurate and a good translation for serious study. A paraphrase version does not contain the exact word-by-word translation of Scriptures.

SECOND:

There are more study tools available for the King James version. There are a large number of concordances, dictionaries, and commentaries written for the King James text.

THIRD:

The King James version is available in more languages than any other version. Since Harvestime International Institute courses are used throughout the world, we selected this version of the Bible because it is available in many languages. It is important to have a Bible in your native tongue because you think and understand best in your own language.

If you do not have a King James version of the Bible write to the American Bible Society at P.O. Box 5601, Grand Central Station, New York, New York 10164, U.S.A. They have a complete listing of all the languages in which the King James version of the Bible is available. If you find the King James Version is not available in your language or have difficulty in obtaining a Bible, write to the United Bible Societies, Bible House, P.O. Box 755, Stuttgart 1, Germany. They maintain a list of "Scriptures of the World" which identifies all the languages in the world in which at least one book of the Bible has been published.

If you read English but have a limited vocabulary, you may be interested in obtaining the "Bible in Basic English." This is the entire Old and New Testament written in English using only a basic 1,000 word vocabulary. Write to Cambridge University Press, New York, New York, U.S.A. for further information.

RED LETTER EDITIONS

Several versions of the Bible come in what are called "red letter editions." In red letter editions of the Bible the words of Jesus are printed in red. The rest of the text of the Bible is printed in black ink.

If a red letter edition of the King James version is available in your language, we suggest you obtain it. What Jesus taught is one of the major focuses of Harvestime International Institute training and a red-letter edition emphasizes His teachings.

A SUMMARY

The following chart summarizes how the various versions of the Bible developed:

The Bible:
Inspired By God

▮

Revealed To Holy Men Who Wrote God's Words
In Greek, Hebrew, Aramaic

▮

Interpreted Into Various Languages
Resulting In

▮

Exact Translations And Paraphrase Versions Of The Bible

SELF-TEST

1. Write the Key Verse from memory.

   _____

   _____

   _____

2. What does the word "version" mean?

   _____

3. What is the difference between a translation and a paraphrase version of the Bible?

   _____

   _____

4. What version of the Bible is used in this course?

   _____

5. Why is no translation of the Bible exact?

   _____

   _____

6. What are the three languages in which the Bible was originally written?

   _____

   _____

   _____

(Answers to tests are provided at the conclusion of the final chapter in this manual.)

FOR FURTHER STUDY

We have selected the text of John 3:16 to illustrate the difference between the different versions of the Bible. The versions listed are the most popular English versions of the Bible.

King James Version: For God so loved the world that He gave his only begotten Son that whosoever believeth in Him should not perish but have everlasting life.

New King James Version: For God so loved the world that He gave His only begotten Son, that whoever believes in Him should not perish but have everlasting life.

Revised Standard Version: For God so loved the world that He gave His only Son, that whoever believes in Him should not perish but have eternal life.

Living Bible: For God loved the world so much that He gave His only Son so that anyone who believes in Him shall not perish but have eternal life.

New American Standard Bible: For God so loved the world, that He gave His only begotten Son, that whoever believes in Him should not perish, but have eternal life.

New English Bible: God loved the world so much that He gave His only Son, that everyone who has faith in Him may not die but have eternal life.

Amplified Version: For God so greatly loved and dearly prized the world that He (even) gave up His only-begotten (unique) Son, so that whoever believes in (trusts, clings to, relies on) Him shall not perish-come to destruction, be lost-but have eternal (everlasting) life.

Phillips: For God loved the world so much that He gave His only Son, so that everyone who believes in Him should not be lost, but should have eternal life.

Wurst: For in such a manner did God love the world, insomuch that His Son, the uniquely-begotten One, He gave, in order that everyone who places his trust in Him may not perish but may be having life eternal.

Moffat: For God loved the world so dearly that He gave up His only Son, so that everyone who believes in Him may have eternal life instead of perishing.

CHAPTER FOUR

AN INTRODUCTION TO OUTLINING

OBJECTIVES:

Upon completion of this chapter you will be able to:

- Write the Key Verse from memory.
- Define the term "outline."
- Read an outline.
- Create an outline.

KEY VERSE:

Moreover He said unto me, Son of man, all my words that I shall speak unto thee receive in thine heart and hear with thine ears. (Ezekiel 3:10)

INTRODUCTION

"*Basic Bible Survey I*" includes an outline of each Old Testament book of the Bible. The outlines provide an overview of the general content of God's Word. More detailed outlines are given in "*Basic Bible Survey II*" for the Gospels, Acts, and the Epistles due to the special focus of Harvestime International Institute. The Institute emphasizes what Jesus taught and the results when His teachings were put into action in the early church.

The outlines in this course summarize only the general content of each book of the Bible. When you complete this general survey you should go back and study each book in more detail. These outlines are only a starting point for you to develop more detailed notes for each book of the Bible. To do this you must know how to create a proper outline.

OUTLINING

An outline is a method of organizing study notes. It puts information in summary form for use in future ministry and study. An outline helps you "hear with your ear and receive in your heart" the Word of God (Ezekiel 3:10). An outline centers on a selected subject. This subject becomes the title of the outline. We have used the names of Bible books as outline titles in this course because they are the subjects of study.

The main points in the outline tell something about the subject. There are also sub-points which tell something about the main points. The prefix "sub" means they relate to (tell something about) the main point. They provide more detailed information about the main points.

There are many ways to outline. We have selected one which uses special numbers called Roman numerals for the main points. If you are not familiar with Roman numerals a list is provided in the "For Further Study" section of this chapter. Subpoints on the outline are shown with capital letters of the alphabet. If there are further points under these, they are shown with regular numbers.

Study the following example of an outline:

The Title Is Placed Here

I. This is the Roman numeral for 1 used for the first main point.

    A. This is a capital letter used for a subpoint relating to the main point.
        1. If there was a further subpoint relating to this, it would be marked with the number 1.
        2. If there are other points relating back to subpoint A, continue to place them in numerical order.

    B. Main point I may have several subpoints. If so, continue down through the alphabet using capital letters in order. Each one of these should relate to the main point.

II. To present another main point, use the next Roman numeral.

    A. Subpoints follow the same pattern under every main point.

EXPANDING THE OUTLINES

As an example of how you can expand the general outlines given in this course, we have selected Romans 12:1-2. First read the verses:

I beseech you therefore, brethren, by the mercies of God, that ye present your bodies a living sacrifice holy, acceptable unto God, which is your reasonable service.

And be not conformed to this world; but be ye transformed by the renewing of your mind, that ye may prove what is that good and acceptable, and perfect will of God. (Romans 12:1-2)

Here is the outline developed from the verses:

Steps For Finding God's Will

I. Present your bodies a living sacrifice:

    A. Holy.
    B. Acceptable unto God.

II. Be not conformed to this world:

    A. Be transformed.

        1. We are transformed by the renewing of our minds.

III. These steps will help us prove or find the will of God which is:

    A. Good.
    B. Acceptable.
    C. Perfect.

You can see how this outline clearly summarizes the steps to God's will given in Romans 12:1-2.

You will never complete your outline study of God's Word. The Holy Spirit will constantly give you new understanding about the Word which you will want to add to your outlines.

SELF-TEST

1. Write the Key Verse from memory.

   _____

   _____

   _____

2. What is an outline?

   _____

   _____

   _____

3. Turn to the outline on Genesis in this study. Can you read and understand the information in this outline form?

   _____

4. How are the main points on an outline indicated?

   _____

   _____

   _____

5. How are subpoints under a main point indicated?

   _____

   _____

(Answers to tests are provided at the conclusion of the final chapter in this manual.)

FOR FURTHER STUDY

1. Subpoints are where you can add details to expand the simple outlines given in this course. For example, turn to the outline on the book of Daniel on page 174. The first main point is entitled "Introductory Background: The Reasons for Daniel's Prosperity" and covers chapter 1 verses 1-21. Read through these verses and identify the reasons for his success. List these as subpoints under this main point.

2. The following list of Roman Numerals will assist you in creating and expanding outlines:

Numbers	Roman Numerals
1	I
2	II
3	III
4	IV
5	V
6	VI
7	VII
8	VIII
9	IX
10	X
11	XI
12	XII
13	XIII
14	XIV
15	XV
16	XVI
17	XVII
18	XVIII
19	XIX
20	XX
30	XXX
40	XL
50	L
60	LX
70	LXX
80	LXXX
90	XC
100	C

THE OLD TESTAMENT

INTRODUCTION TO THE BOOKS OF LAW

In previous chapters you learned that the Bible is the written Word of God. You learned it is divided into two major sections called the Old Testament and the New Testament. You learned the four divisions of the Old Testament books: Law, History, Poetry, Prophecy. You also learned the four divisions of the New Testament books: Gospels, History, Letters, and Prophecy.

With this lesson you begin a basic survey of the books which make up the major divisions you have learned about. There are 39 books in the Old Testament. We will start our survey with the books of law:

THE BOOKS OF LAW

The books of law were written by Moses and they span a period of 600 years. The books of law consist of five books:

Genesis: Records the beginning of the universe, man, the Sabbath, marriage, sin, sacrifice, nations, and government. Also records the stories of key men of God: Abraham, Isaac, Jacob, and Joseph.

Exodus: Details how Israel became a nation with Moses as leader. Israel is delivered from bondage in Egypt and journeys to Mt. Sinai where the law of God is given.

Leviticus: This book was a manual of worship for Israel. It provides instruction to the religious leaders and explains how a sinful people can approach a righteous God. It points also to the coming of Jesus Christ as the Lamb of God who takes away the sins of the world.

Numbers: Records Israel's 40 years of wandering in the wilderness as a result of disobedience to God. The title of the book is from two "numberings" or population census taken during the long journey.

Deuteronomy: Records the close of Moses' life and reviews the laws given in Exodus and Leviticus.

CHAPTER FIVE

GENESIS

OBJECTIVES:

Upon completion of this chapter you will be able to:
- Name the author of the book of Genesis.
- Identify to whom the book of Genesis was written.
- State the purpose for the book of Genesis.
- Write the Key Verse of the book of Genesis from memory.
- State the Life and Ministry Principle for the book of Genesis.

INTRODUCTION

AUTHOR: Moses

TO WHOM: Israel

PURPOSE: To preserve the historical background of Israel and the record of creation, sin, redemption, and God's first dealings with man.

KEY VERSE: Genesis 3:15

LIFE AND MINISTRY PRINCIPLES: God's plan from the beginning included all nations. God begins new things with people.

MAIN CHARACTERS: Adam, Eve, Cain, Abel, Enoch, Esau, Jacob (Israel), Enoch, Abraham, Isaac, Joseph

OUTLINE

I. The history of humanity: 1:1-11:26

    A. Creation: 1:1-2:25
    B. The fall of man: 3:1-4:26
        1. Adam and Eve: 3:1-24
        2. Cain and Abel: 4:1-26
    C. Genealogy from the fall to the flood: 5:1-32
    D. The flood: 6:1-9:29

        1. The wickedness of man: 6:1-4
        2. God's decision: 6:5-7
        3. Noah: 6:8-10
        4. God speaks to Noah: 6:11-21
        5. Noah's response: 6:22
        6. God speaks to Noah: 7:1-4
        7. Noah's response: 7:5-16
        8. Life in the ark: 7:17-24
        9. Release from the ark: 8:1-19
        10. God's covenant: 9:1-17
        11. Generations of Noah: 9:18-19
        12. Sins of Noah's family: 9:20-29
   E. From the flood to Abraham: 10:1-11:26
        1. Generations of the sons of Noah: 10:1-32
        2. The tower of Babel: 11:1-9
        3. Generations of Shem: 11:10-26
        4. Generations of Terah: 11:27-32

II. The patriarchal history of Israel: 11:27-50:26

   A. Abraham: 11:27-25:10
        1. Abraham's birth and ancestry: 11:26-30
        2. His wanderings: 11:31-13:1
           (a) From Ur to Haran: 11:31-32
           (b) From Haran to Canaan: 12:1-9
           (c) To Egypt and back: 12:10-13:1
        3. Abraham and Lot: 13:2-14:24
           (a) Dispute and division: 13:2-13
           (b) God's promise to Abraham: 13:14-18
           (c) Lot captured by the kings of the east: 14:1-24
        4. The covenant: 15:1-20
        5. Ishmael: 16:1-16
        6. Circumcision: 17:1-27
        7. A promised son: 18:1-15
        8. Sodom and Gomorrah: 18:16-19:38
        9. Abraham visits Abimelech: 20:1-18
        10. Isaac born and Ishmael driven out: 21:1-21
        11. Abraham and Abimelech: 21:22-34
        12. Proposed sacrifice of Isaac: 22:1-19
        13. The death and burial of Sarah: 23:1-20
        14. Marriage of Isaac and Rebekah: 24:1-67
        15. Abraham and Keturah: 25:1-6
        16. Abraham's death and burial 25:7-10

B. Isaac: 25:11-35:29
   1. Birth of Isaac: 21:1-8
   2. Marriage to Rebekah: 24
   3. Isaac and his sons: 25:19-35:29
   4. Covenant renewed: 26:1-5
   5. Deception of Abimelech: 26:6-33
   6. Marriage to Judith and Bashemath: 26:34-35
   7. Isaac deceived by Jacob: 27:1-45
   8. Jacob's flight to Haran: 27:46-28:5
   9. Death of Isaac: 35:27-29
C. Jacob: 28:10-36:43
   1. His birth: 25:19-26
   2. Rivalry between Jacob and Esau: 25:27-45
      (a) The birthright: 25:27-34
      (b) The blessing: 27:1-45
   3. The flight to Haran: 27:46-29:14
   4. Jacob's marriages to Leah and Rachel: 29:15-30
   5. Life in Haran: 29:31-30:43
   6. Return to Canaan: 31:1-55
   7. Preparations to meet Esau: 32:1-23
   8. Jacob's wrestling match: 32:24-32
   9. Peace with Esau: 33:1-17
   10. Jacob and his family in Canaan: 33:18-45:28
   11. Jacob's final days and death: 46:1-50:14
D. Joseph: 37:1-50:26
   1. Joseph's early life: 37:1-36
      (a) His coat: 37:1-4
      (b) His dreams: 37:5-11
      (c) Sold into slavery: 37:12-36
      (d) The sin of Judah: 38:1-30
   2. Joseph the slave: 39:1-40:23
      (a) In Potiphar's house: 39:1-20
      (b) In prison: 39:21-40:23
   3. Joseph the prime minister: 41:1-45:28
      (a) Preparation for famine: 41:1-57
      (b) Joseph and his brothers: 42:1-45:28
      (c) Joseph and his family in Egypt: 46:1-50:21
      (d) Joseph's death: 50:22-26

SELF-TEST

1. Who was the author of the book of Genesis?

   _____

2. State the purpose for the book of Genesis.

   _____

   _____

   _____

3. To whom was the book of Genesis written?

   _____

   _____

4. State the Life and Ministry Principles of the book of Genesis.

   _____

   _____

   _____

5. Write the Key Verse of Genesis.

   _____

   _____

   _____

(Answers to tests are provided at the conclusion of the final chapter in this manual.)

FOR FURTHER STUDY

1. The name "Genesis" means beginnings. This book contains the record of the beginning of:

    -The world: 1:1-25
    -Humanity: 1:26-2
    -Sin: 3:1-7
    -Salvation: 3:8-24
    -Families: 4:1-15
    -Civilization: 4:16-9
    -Nations: 10:1-11:32
    -The Jewish nation: 12:50

2. Genesis is divided into two major segments: Chapters 1-11 cover four major events. Chapters 12-50 cover four major people.

3. Study chapters 1-2 and complete the following chart:

Day	What God Created
1	
2	
3	
4	
5	
6	
7	

4. In chapters 3-9 what do you learn about the following:

    -Tactics of the enemy (Satan...the serpent):_____
    -Eve's progression into sin:_____
    -The consequences of sin entering the world:_____
    -God's judgment by the flood:_____

5. For chapters 12-50: Identify the four major characters and study their lives in depth, drawing spiritual applications to your own life. Also study the word "covenant" which is used extensively in this section.

CHAPTER SIX

EXODUS

OBJECTIVES

Upon completion of this chapter you will be able to:

- Name the author of the book of Exodus.
- Identify to whom the book of Exodus was written.
- State the purpose for the book of Exodus.
- Write the Key Verse of the book of Exodus from memory.
- State the Life and Ministry Principle for the book of Exodus.

INTRODUCTION

AUTHOR: Moses

TO WHOM: Israel

PURPOSE: To record the deliverance of Israel from slavery and document their purpose for existence as a nation.

KEY VERSE: Exodus 12:13

LIFE AND MINISTRY PRINCIPLE: Salvation comes only through the blood of the Lamb of God, Jesus.

MAIN CHARACTERS: Moses, Aaron, Pharaoh, Miriam, Jethro

OUTLINE

I. The nation of Israel in Egypt: 1:1-12:36

    A. Egyptian bondage: 1:1-22
    B. God prepares a deliverer: Moses: 2:1-4:31
    C. The dialogue with Pharaoh: 5:1-11:10
    D. The Passover: 12:1-30

      E.   Deliverance from Egypt: 12:31-36

II.   Israel in the wilderness: 12:37-18:27

      A.   The Exodus and the pursuit by the Egyptians: 12:37-15:21
      B.   The journey to Sinai: 15:22-17:16
      C.   The visit of Jethro: 18:1-27

III.   Israel at Sinai: 19:1-40:38

      A.   The giving of the law: 19:1-25
      B.   Laws governing moral life: 19-22
      C.   Laws governing social life: 22-23
      D.   Laws governing religious life: 24:1-31:18
      E.   The tabernacle: 24:12-40:38
           1.   The tabernacle designed: Instructions concerning the tabernacle and the priests: 24:12-31:18
           2.   The tabernacle delayed: The golden calf and renewal of the covenant: 32:1-34:35
           3.   The tabernacle completed: Erection of the tabernacle and institution of the priesthood: 35:1-40:38

SELF-TEST

1. Who was the author of the book of Exodus?

2. State the purpose for the book of Exodus.

3. To whom was the book of Exodus written?

4. State the Life and Ministry Principle of the book of Exodus.

5. Write the Key Verse of Exodus.

(Answers to tests are provided at the conclusion of the final chapter in this manual.)

FOR FURTHER STUDY

1. God sent ten plagues on Egypt in the process of making Pharaoh willing to release Israel from slavery:

   -Blood: 7:14-25
   -Frogs: 8:1-15
   -Lice: 8:16-19
   -Flies: 8:20-32
   -Murrain: 9:1-7
   -Boils: 9:8-12
   -Hail: 9:13-35
   -Locusts: 10:1-20
   -Darkness: 10:21-29
   -Death: 11:1-10, 12:29-36

2. Exodus 20:1-17 records the best known of Old Testament law, the Ten Commandments.

3. One of the important subjects in Exodus is the plan for the tabernacle. The diagram on the next page shows the plan God gave Moses for this holy place of worship.

   The tabernacle was important because it was the place of worship and sacrifice for Israel, but the tabernacle was also a spiritual type. This means that each part of the tabernacle was symbolic of a greater spiritual truth.

   The courtyard around the tabernacle measured 150 feet by 75 feet. It is a symbol of the world.

   The altar of burnt offering was 7 1/2 feet square and 4 1/2 feet high. Sacrifices were burned here which symbolized the sacrifice of Jesus for the sins of the world.

   The laver was a large basin where the priests washed their hands and feet before going into the Holy Place. It is a symbol of Christian baptism.

   The Holy Place measured 30 by 15 feet. It symbolizes the church separated from the world (the court) and entered by way of Christ's sacrifice (the altar) and baptism (the laver).

   The table of shewbread is a symbol of the Lord's Supper (or communion, as it is called in some denominations).

The candlestick provided light for the Holy Place. It is a symbol of God's Word.

The altar of incense was the place where incense was burned. The sweet smelling smoke ascended to God as a symbol of the prayers of His people.

The veil was a curtain between the Holy Place and the Most Holy Place. It symbolized the separation between God and man.

The Most Holy Place was 15 feet long, wide, and high. It was a perfect cube shape and is a symbol of heaven. It was the dwelling place of God's presence.

The ark of the covenant was a wooden chest covered with gold. It had a lid decorated with two golden cherubim. The ark contained the Ten Commandments which symbolized God's government, a dish of manna which recalled God's provision, and Aaron's rod which was a reminder of God's power among His people. Once a year the high priest sprinkled the top of the ark with blood which was a symbol of Christ's blood by which we are cleansed from sin.

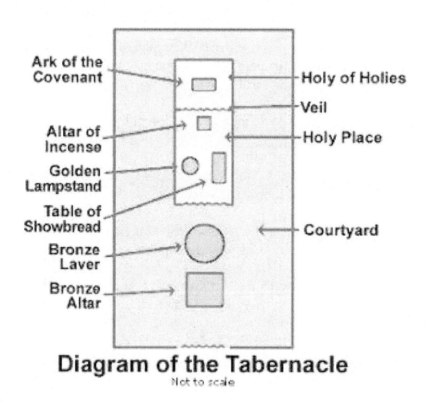

Diagram of the Tabernacle
Not to scale

Holy Days

Study the references in Column One and complete the chart. The first one is done as an example for you to follow. These are the Holy Days which God ordained for the nation of Israel to observe.

Passages	Holy Days	Date	Purpose Of Observance
Leviticus 23:3 Exodus 20:8-11 Deuteronomy 5:12-15	Sabbath	7th Day Weekly	Rest from labor; worship
Leviticus 23:5 Numbers 28:16 Deuteronomy 16:1-2	Passover	1/14	
Leviticus 23:6-8 Numbers 28:17-25 Deuteronomy 16:3-8	Unleavened Bread	1/15-21	
Leviticus 23:9-14 Exodus 23:16 Numbers 28:26-31	First fruits	1/16	
Leviticus 23:15-22 Exodus 34:22 Deuteronomy 16:9-12	Pentecost	3/6	
Leviticus 23:23-25 Numbers 29:1-6	Trumpets	7/1	
Leviticus 23:26-32 Leviticus 16 Numbers 29:7-11	Day Of Atonement	7/10	
Leviticus 23:33-44 Numbers 29:12-40 Deuteronomy 16:13-15	Tabernacles	7/15-21	

Passages	Holy Days	Date	Purpose Of Observance
Leviticus 25:1-7 Exodus 23:10-11	Sabbatical Year	Every 7th Year	
Leviticus 25:8-55	Jubilee	Every 50th Year	

CHAPTER SEVEN

LEVITICUS

OBJECTIVES:

Upon completion of this chapter you will be able to:

- Name the author of the book of Leviticus.
- Identify to whom the book of Leviticus was written.
- State the purpose for the book of Leviticus.
- Write the Key Verse of the book of Leviticus from memory.
- State the Life and Ministry Principle for the book of Leviticus.

INTRODUCTION

AUTHOR: Moses

TO WHOM: Israel

PURPOSE: To show Israel how to live as a holy nation in fellowship with God and prepare them to extend the redemptive plan of God to all nations.

KEY VERSE: Leviticus 20:7

LIFE AND MINISTRY PRINCIPLE: God requires holiness of His people.

MAIN CHARACTERS: Moses, Aaron

OUTLINE

I. Laws concerning sacrifices: 1:1-7:38

    A. Introduction: 1:1-2
    B. The burnt offering: 1:3-17
    C. The meal offering: 2:1-16
    D. The peace offering: 3:1-17
    E. The sin offering: 4:1-5:13
    F. The trespass offering: 5:14-17

II. Laws and incidents concerning the priests: 8-10

    A. Prescriptions for consecration: 8:1-9:24
    B. Punishment for violation: 10:1-20

III. Laws of purification: 11:1-15:33

    A. Clean and unclean food: 11:1-47
    B. Purification after childbirth: 12:1-8
    C. Leprosy: 13:1-14:57
    D. Sexual impurities and cleansings: 15:1-33

IV. The day of Atonement: 16:1-34

    A. Aaron's preparation: 16:1-10
    B. The sin offering for the priests: 16:11-14
    C. The sin offering for the people: 16:15-19
    D. The scapegoat: 16:20-22
    E. The offering completed: 16:23-28
    F. The solemnity of the day: 16:29-34

V. The holiness code: 17:1-27:34

    A. Prohibitions: 17:1-22:33
        1. Holiness on the part of the people: 17:1-20:27
        2. Holiness on the part of the priests: 21:1-22:33
    B. Religious festivals: 23:1-44
        1. The Sabbath: 23:1-3
        2. Passover and unleavened bread: 23:4-14
        3. Feast of weeks, or Pentecost: 23:15-22
        4. Feast of trumpets: 23:23-25
        5. Day of Atonement: 23:25-32
        6. Feast of tabernacles: 23:33-44
    C. Religious symbols: 24:1-23
    D. Sabbatic year and jubilee: 25:1-26:2
    E. Promises and warnings: 26:3-46
        1. The necessity for right relationship to God: 26:1-2
        2. The blessings of obedience to God: 26:1-2
        3. The chastisements for disobedience: 26:14-39
        4. God's faithfulness to His covenant: 26:40-45
        5. Summary statement: 26:46
    F. Vows and tithes: 27:1-34
        1. Vows to persons: 27:2-8

2. Vows of domestic animals: 27:9-1.
3. Vows of houses and fields: 27:14-25
4. The tithe: 27:30-33
    (a) First among beasts: 27:26-27
    (b) Devoted things: 27:28-29
    (c) The tithe: 27:30-33

SELF-TEST

1. Who was the author of the book of Leviticus?

   _____

2. State the purpose for the book of Leviticus.

   _____

   _____

   _____

3. To whom was the book of Leviticus written?

   _____

   _____

4. State the Life and Ministry Principle of the book of Leviticus.

   _____

   _____

   _____

5. Write the Key Verse of Leviticus.

   _____

   _____

   _____

(Answers to tests are provided at the conclusion of the final chapter in this manual.)

FOR FURTHER STUDY

1. Study the word "holy" in Leviticus. It is used over 100 times. Other key words are "sacrifice" used 42 times, "priest" used 189 times, and "blood" used 86 times.

2. The standard of holiness described in Leviticus is both vertical and horizontal. It is vertical in the message of chapters 1-10 ("I am holy") and horizontal in the message of chapters 11-27 ("Be ye holy").

I Am Holy
Chapters 1-10

↔

Be Ye Holy
Chapters 11-27

3. There are five different offerings described in Leviticus. The first three offerings were instituted to maintain fellowship with God. The last two were to restore broken fellowship.

Offering	Chapter Were It Is Introduced	Laws Detailed
Burnt	1	6:8-13
Meal	2	6:14-23
Peace	3	7:11-34
Sin	4	6:25-30
Trespass	5:1-6:7	7:1-7

4. The number seven (7) has great significance in the book of Leviticus:
-Every 7th day was a Sabbath.
-Blood was sprinkled 7 times in the tabernacle.
-Every 7th year was a Sabbatic year.
-Every 7th Sabbatic year was followed by a Jubilee year.
-Every 7th month was especially holy, having three feasts.
-There were 7 weeks between Passover and Pentecost.
-The Passover feast lasted 7 days.
-Unclean persons were isolated 7 days.
-The Feast of Tabernacles lasted 7 days.
-At Passover, 14 lambs (2 x 7) were offered daily.
-At Pentecost 7 lambs were offered.
-At the feast of tabernacles 14 lambs were offered daily.

CHAPTER EIGHT

NUMBERS

OBJECTIVES:

Upon completion of this chapter you will be able to:

- Name the author of the book of Numbers.
- Identify to whom the book of Numbers was written.
- State the purpose for the book of Numbers.
- Write the Key Verse of the book of Numbers from memory.
- State the Life and Ministry Principle for the book of Numbers.

INTRODUCTION

AUTHOR: Moses

TO WHOM: Israel

PURPOSE: Records experiences of the wilderness journey which are a type of the defeated Christian.

KEY VERSE: Numbers 32:23

LIFE AND MINISTRY PRINCIPLE: God is not pleased with anything less than total commitment.

MAIN CHARACTERS: Moses, Korah, Balaam, Aaron, Miriam, Joshua, Caleb

OUTLINE

I. Preparation for departure from Sinai: 1:1-10:10

    A. The people numbered: 1:1-54
    B. The camp arranged: 2:1-34
    C. The priest and Levites instructed: 3:1-4:49
    D. The people protected: 5:1-31
    E. The vow of the Nazarite: 6:1-27
    F. Gifts of the princes: 7:1-89
    G. Lighting of the tabernacle lamps: 8:1-4

      H.   Cleansing of the Levites: 8:5-26
      I.   Observance of the Passover: 9:1-14
      J.   Guidance of the camp: 9:15-23
      K.   Calling an assembly and moving the camp: 10:1-10

II.   The journey from Mt. Sinai to Kadesh-Barnea: 10:11-12:15

      A.   Mobilizing for the march: 10:11-28
      B.   Hobab refuses service: 10:29-32
      C.   A continuing cloud: 10:34-36
      D.   A fiery judgment: 11:1-3
      E.   A murmuring multitude: 11:4-9
      F.   A provoked prophet: 11:10-15
      G.   A deadly diet: 11:31-34
      H.   A suffering sister: 12:1-15

III.   Israel at Kadesh-Barnea: 13:1-14:45

      A.   Spying out the land: 13:1-25
      B.   The reports and response: 13:26-14:10
      C.   The judgment of God: 14:11-34

IV.   Events during the wilderness wandering: 20:1-35:34

      A.   Stoning of a Sabbath breaker: 15:32-36
      B.   The rebellion of Korah: 16:1-32
      C.   The budding of Aaron's rod: 17:1-13
      D.   Instructions to Aaron: 18:1-19:22
      E.   The death of Miriam: 20:1
      F.   The sin of Moses: 20:1-13
      G.   A request refused: 20:14-22
      H.   Aaron's death: 20:23-29
      I.   Serpents among the people: 21:5-9
      J.   A perverted prophet: 22:1-24:25
      K.   A patriotic priest: 25:1-18
      L.   Miscellaneous instructions: 26:1-31:54
      M.   Territorial distribution in East Jordan: 32:1-42
      N.   Record of the journey from Egypt: 33:1-56
      O.   Instructions prior to entering Canaan: 34:1-36:13

SELF-TEST

1. Who was the author of the book of Numbers?

   _____

2. State the purpose for the book of Numbers.

   _____

   _____

   _____

3. To whom was the book of Numbers written?

   _____

   _____

4. State the Life and Ministry Principle of the book of Numbers.

   _____

   _____

   _____

5. Write the Key Verse of Numbers.

   _____

   _____

   _____

(Answers to tests are provided at the conclusion of the final chapter in this manual.)

FOR FURTHER STUDY

1. Changes in leadership of Israel occur in Numbers. Joshua replaces Moses as the political leader and Eleazar succeeds Aaron as the religious leader: See Numbers 27:15-23 and 20:23-29.

2. The death and resurrection of Jesus are illustrated in Numbers by a serpent and a stick: 21:5-9; 17:8

3. The following chart records the results of the two "numberings" or census of Israel:

Tribe	**First Census**	**Second Census**
Reuben	46,500	43,730
Simeon	59,300	22,200
Gad	45,650	40,500
Judah	74,600	76,500
Issachar	54,400	64,300
Zebulun	57,400	60,500
Ephriam	40,500	32,500
Manasseh	32,200	52,700
Benjamin	35,400	45,600
Dan	62,700	64,400
Asher	41,500	53,400
Naphtali	53,400	45,400
Total	**603,550**	**601,730**

4. This diagram shows the arrangement of the camps of the tribes of Israel in relation to the tabernacle.

North

```
x x x x x x x x x x x x x x x x x x x x x x x x x x x x x x x x x x x x x x x x x x x x
x                                                                                       x
x       Asher               Dan                     Naphtali                            x
x                                                                                       x
x                   x x x x x x x x x x x x x x x                                       x
x       Benjamin    x                             x         Issachar                    x
x                   x       Merarites             x                                     x
x                   x                             x                                     x
x       Ephraim     x       Gershonites  Moses    x                                     x
x                   x                    Aaron    x         Judah                       x
x                   x       _____   Priests  x                                     x
x                   x                             x                                     x
x                   x       Tabernacle            x                                     x
x                   x       _____            x                                     x
x                   x                             x                                     x
x                   x       Kohathites            x                                     x
x       Manasseh    x x x x x x x x x x x x x x x           Zebulun                     x
x                                                                                       x
x       Gad                 Reuben                          Simeon                      x
x                                                                                       x
x x x x x x x x x x x x x x x x x x x x x x x x x x x x x x x x x x x x x x x x x x x x x
```

South

71

CHAPTER NINE

DEUTERONOMY

OBJECTIVES:

Upon completion of this chapter you will be able to:

- Name the author of the book of Deuteronomy.
- Identify to whom the book of Deuteronomy was written.
- State the purpose for the book of Deuteronomy.
- Write the Key Verses of the book of Deuteronomy from memory.
- State the Life and Ministry Principle for the book of Deuteronomy.

INTRODUCTION

AUTHOR: Moses

TO WHOM: Israel

PURPOSE: To restate the law to the new generations of Israelites born since Mt. Sinai.

KEY VERSES: Deuteronomy 6:4-5

LIFE AND MINISTRY PRINCIPLE: Obedience brings blessing. Disobedience brings judgment.

MAIN CHARACTERS: Moses, Joshua, Balaam, Amalek, Miriam

OUTLINE

I. Moses' first sermon: Historical 1:1-4

    A. Historical introduction: 1:1-5
    B. Review of the journey from Horeb to Moab: 1:6-3:29
    C. Appeal to the new generation to keep the law: 4:1-40
    D. Account of the appointment of the cities of refuge: 4:41-43
    E. Summary of the law of Moses: 4:44-49

II. Moses' second sermon: Legal 5:1-26:19

    A. The ten commandments are repeated: 5:7-21
    B. He warns against immorality (23:17); compromise (7:1-5); and witchcraft: 18:9-14
    C. Moses describes Canaan: 8:7-8
    D. He reviews his personal experiences with God on Mt. Sinai: 9:9-21
    E. He reminds them of their financial obligations to God: 26:1-19
    F. Laws concerning clothing (22:50; divorce (24:1-4); women's rights (21:10-17; 22:13-20); and warfare (20:1-20) are given.
    G. He summarizes God's plan: 6:23

III. Moses' third sermon: Prophetic: 27:1-30:20

    A. Inscription of laws on stone, and blessings and curses: 27:1-26
    B. Prediction of blessings and curses: 28:1-68
    C. Exhortations to holiness: 29:1-30:20

IV. Historical appendix: 31:1-34:12

    A. Moses' final words and appointment of Joshua: 31:1-30
    B. Moses' song and exhortation: 32:1-47
    C. God's final words to Moses: 32:48-52
    D. Moses' parting blessing on the tribes: 33:1-29
    E. The death and burial of Moses: 34:1-12

SELF-TEST

1. Who was the author of the book of Deuteronomy?

   _____

2. State the purpose for the book of Deuteronomy:

   _____

   _____

   _____

3. To whom was the book of Deuteronomy written?

   _____

   _____

4. State the Life and Ministry Principle of the book of Deuteronomy.

   _____

   _____

   _____

5. Write the Key Verses of Deuteronomy.

   _____

   _____

   _____

   _____

(Answers to tests are provided at the conclusion of the final chapter in this manual.)

FOR FURTHER STUDY

1. Jesus quoted from the book of Deuteronomy during His temptation by Satan. Compare Matthew 4:4 with Deuteronomy 8:3; Matthew 4:7 with Deuteronomy 6:16; and Matthew 4:10 with Deuteronomy 6:13.

2. Deuteronomy is a historical book, but it contains four important prophecies:

    -The entrance of Israel under Joshua into Canaan: 7:2; 9:1-3; 31:3,5
    -The sin of Israel while in Canaan: 31:16-18, 20, 29
    -The exile from Canaan: 4:26-28; 7:4; 8:19-20; 28:36,41,49,50,53,64
    -The return of Israel back to Canaan: 4:29; 30:1-3,10

3. Study the key words "do," "keep," and "observe." They are found 177 times in Deuteronomy.

4. Another key word of this book is "remember." It is frequently repeated throughout the entire book. The Israelites are told to remember:

    -The giving of the Law: 4:9-10
    -The covenant: 4:23
    -Their past slavery: 5:15
    -Their deliverance: 7:18
    -God's leadership and provision: 8:2-6
    -Sins of the past: 9:7
    -Judgments of God: 24:9
    -The days of old: 32:7

5. This book contains a song that may be sung during the great tribulation. Compare Deuteronomy 31:30-32:45 with Revelation 15:3-4.

6. A major theme of Deuteronomy is the importance of the Word of God. See 4:1, 2, 7, 9; 6:7-9; 11:18-21; 27:1-4; 30:11-14; 31:11-12; 32:46-47.

7. For the historical context of Leviticus, read Numbers 21:21-22:1 and Deuteronomy 1:1-5.

INTRODUCTION TO THE BOOKS OF HISTORY

The next group of books we will survey are the books of history. These include the following books:

Joshua: Details how the successor of Moses, Joshua, led the people of Israel into the Promised Land of Canaan. It records the military campaigns and the division of the land among the people.

Judges: Israel turned away from God after Joshua's death. This book records the sad story of their repeated sins and the judges God raised up to deliver them from enemy forces.

Ruth: The story of Ruth, a woman of the Gentile nation of Moab, who chose to serve the God of Israel. She became the great grandmother of David.

I Samuel: This book centers on three persons: Samuel who was the last of the judges of Israel; Saul, the first king of Israel; and David who succeeded a disobedient Saul as king.

II Samuel: The glorious forty year reign of King David is recorded in this book.

I Kings: King Solomon's reign and the kings of the divided kingdom through the reigns of Ahab in the north and Jehoshaphat in the south are the subjects of this book.

II Kings: The final decline of Israel and Judah is recalled in this book.

I Chronicles: The reign of David and preparations for building the temple are recorded here. The time of this book parallels that of II Samuel.

II Chronicles: This book continues Israel's history through Solomon's reign with focus on the southern kingdom. It closes with the decree of Cyrus which permitted the return of the people from Babylon to Jerusalem.

Ezra: The return of the Jews from Babylon captivity is detailed in this book.

Nehemiah: The rebuilding of Jerusalem's walls under Nehemiah is documented in the book of Nehemiah. This project was begun about fourteen years after Ezra's return with the people.

Esther: God's deliverance of the Jews through Esther and Mordecai is the subject of this book.

CHAPTER TEN

JOSHUA

OBJECTIVES:

Upon completion of this chapter you will be able to:
- Name the author of the book of Joshua.
- Identify to whom the book of Joshua was written.
- State the purpose for the book of Joshua.
- Write the Key Verse of the book of Joshua from memory.
- State the Life and Ministry Principle for the book of Joshua.

INTRODUCTION

AUTHOR: Joshua

TO WHOM: Israel

PURPOSE: Record the history of the conquest of Canaan.

KEY VERSE: Joshua 24:15

LIFE AND MINISTRY PRINCIPLE: No moral or spiritual victories are won without battles.

MAIN CHARACTERS: Joshua, Rahab, Caleb, Achan, Balaam, Eleazar

OUTLINE

I. Entering the land: 1:1-5:15

    A. Joshua commissioned: 1:1-9
    B. Preparation to cross the Jordan: 1:10-2:24
    C. Jordan crossed: 3:1-4:24
    D. Gilgal occupied: 5:1-15

II. Possessing the land: 6:1-12:24

    A. Jericho and Ai taken: 6:1-8:29
    B. Joshua's altar: 8:30-35

- C. The Gibeonites received: 9:1-27
- D. Southern Canaan conquered: 10:1-43
- E. Northern Canaan conquered: 11:1-15
- F. The conquest summarized: 11:16-12:24

III. Occupying the land: 13:1-22:34

- A. Joshua instructed: 13:1-7
- B. The eastern tribes assigned: 13:8-33
- C. The western tribes assigned: 14:1-19:51
- D. The cities of refuge: 20:1-9
- E. Levitical towns: 21:1-45
- F. Eastern tribes sent home: 22:1-34

IV. Joshua's farewell address and death: 23:1-24:33

- A. He reminds them of God's goodness: 23:3-10
- B. He warns them concerning disobedience: 23:11-13
- C. He reviews this history: 24:1-13
- D. He challenges them to serve God: 24:14-18
- E. He completes the book that bears his name: 24:26-28
- F. He dies and departs for Heaven: 24:29-33

SELF-TEST

1. Who was the author of the book of Joshua?

   _____

2. State the purpose for the book of Joshua.

   _____

   _____

3. To whom was the book of Joshua written?

   _____

   _____

4. State the Life and Ministry Principle of the book of Joshua.

   _____

   _____

   _____

5. Write the Key Verse of Joshua.

   _____

   _____

   _____

(Answers to tests are provided at the conclusion of the final chapter in this manual.)

FOR FURTHER STUDY

The book of Joshua can be contrasted to the book of Exodus. In Exodus, God parted the waters of the Red Sea to bring His people out of the land of bondage in Egypt. In Joshua, God parted the waters of the Jordan River to bring His people into Canaan, the land of blessing.

Moses summarized both books in Deuteronomy 6:23:

"And He brought us out...that He might bring us in."

CHAPTER ELEVEN

JUDGES

OBJECTIVES:

Upon completion of this chapter you will be able to:

- Name the author of the book of Judges.
- Identify to whom the book of Judges was written.
- State the purpose for the book of Judges.
- Write the Key Verse of the book of Judges from memory.
- State the Life and Ministry Principle for the book of Judges.

INTRODUCTION

AUTHOR: Samuel

TO WHOM: Israel.

PURPOSE: Historical record of the rule of the judges which occurred after the close of the book of Joshua.

KEY VERSE: Judges 17:6

LIFE AND MINISTRY PRINCIPLE: There is a divine pattern of chastisement designed to turn God's people from sin to salvation.

MAIN CHARACTERS: The judges (See list in outline below)

OUTLINE

I. Introduction to the period of the judges: 1:1-2:5

    A. Political conditions from Joshua to the time of the judges: 1:1-36
    B. Religious conditions from Joshua to the time of the judges: 2:1-5

II. The period of the judges: 2:6-16:31

    A. Summary of religious conditions of the entire period: 2:6-3:6

- B. List of the judges: 3:7-16:31
    1. Othniel of Judah: 3:7-11
    2. Ehud of Benjamin: 3:12-30
    3. Shamgar: 3:31
    4. Deborah of Ephraim and Barak of Naphtali: 4:1-5:31
    5. Gideon of Manasseh and Abimelech: 6:1-9:57
    6. Tola of Issachar: 10:1-2
    7. Jair of Gilead: 10:3-5
    8. Jephthah of Gilead: 10:6-12:7
    9. Ibzan of Zebulon: 12:8-10
    10. Elon of Zebulon: 12:11-12
    11. Abdon of Ephriam: 12:13-15
    12. Samson of Dan: 13:1-16:31

III. Historical appendix: 17:1-21:25

- A. The idolatry of Micah and the Danites: 17:1-18:31
    1. Micah and his personal priest: 17:1-13
    2. The Danites join the idolatry: 18:1-31
- B. The crime of Benjamin at Gibeah and its punishment: 19:1-21:25
    1. The stop in Gibeah: 19:1-15
    2. The crime: 19:16-27
    3. The Levite's response: 19:28-29
    4. The outrage of Israel: 19:30-20:11
    5. The three battle war: 20:12-21:25

SELF-TEST

1. Who was the author of the book of Judges?

   _____

2. State the purpose for the book of Judges.

   _____

   _____

   _____

3. To whom was the book of Judges written?

   _____

   _____

4. State the Life and Ministry Principle of the book of Judges.

   _____

   _____

   _____

5. Write the Key Verse of Judges.

   _____

   _____

   _____

(Answers to tests are provided at the conclusion of the final chapter in this manual.)

FOR FURTHER STUDY

1. The book of Judges is a direct contrast to the book of Joshua.

    Joshua tells of victory, freedom, faith, progress, obedience, spiritual vision, joy, strength, and unity among the tribes with strong leadership.

    Judges describes defeat, slavery, unbelief, division, disobedience, earthly emphasis, sorrow, weakness, and disunity among the tribes.

2. Galatians provides an excellent summary of the books of Joshua and Judges. Galatians 5:22-26 describes Joshua, and 5:17-21 describes Judges.

3. Judges is a classic example of Hosea 8:7 and Galatians 6:7.

4. Judges 17:6 summarizes the conditions which existed in Israel during the period of the Judges.

5. The story of the strongest man in history is found in Judges 15.

6. Read the story of an army which was put to death for mispronouncing a word: Judges 12.

7. God used unusual methods in the book of Judges. He used:

    -An ox goad: 3:31
    -A nail: 4:21
    -Trumpets: 7:20
    -Pitchers: 7:20
    -Lamps: 7:20
    -A millstone: 9:53
    -A jawbone of an ass: 15:15

8. Complete the following chart as you study the recurring cycles of the book of Judges. The first cycle is done as an example for you to follow:

The Cycle Of Judges

Cycles	3:7-11	3:12-30	4:1-5:31	6:1-8:32	8:33-10:5	10:6-12:15	13:1-16:31
S I N	Idolatry						
S E R V I C E	8 years King of Mesopotamia						
S U P P L I C A T I O N	Cried unto the Lord						
S A L V A T I O N	Othniel by war						
S I L E N C E	40 years						

Judges Of Israel

Name	Dates B.C	Number of Years
Othniel	1400-1360	40
Ehud	1360-1280	80
Shamgar	1280	1
Deborah	1280-1240	40
Gideon	1240-1200	40
Abimelech	1200-1197	3
Tola	1197-1174	23
Jair	1174-1152	22
Jephthah	1152-1146	6
Ibzan	1146-1138	8
Elon	1138-1128	10
Abdon	1128-1121	7
Samson	1121-1101	20

CHAPTER TWELVE
RUTH

OBJECTIVES:

Upon completion of this chapter you will be able to:

- Name the author of the book of Ruth.
- Identify to whom the book of Ruth was written.
- State the purpose for the book of Ruth.
- Write the Key Verses of the book of Ruth from memory.
- State the Life and Ministry Principle for the book of Ruth.

INTRODUCTION

AUTHOR: Unknown

TO WHOM: Israel

PURPOSE: Written as part of the historical record of Israel to illustrate the concern of God for all people. It also illustrates the kinsman-redeemer relationship of Jesus Christ.

KEY VERSES: Ruth 1:16-17

LIFE AND MINISTRY PRINCIPLE: God can turn bitterness to blessing.

MAIN CHARACTERS: Naomi (Mara), Elimelech, Mahlon, Chilion, Orpha, Ruth, Boaz, an unnamed kinsman.

OUTLINE

I. Moab: 1:1-5

    A. Journey to Moab: 1:1-2
        1. When the story occurs: 1:1
        2. Why they went to Moab: 1:1
        3. Introduction of the family: 1:2

    B. Tragedy in Moab: 1:3-5
        1. Naomi's husband dies: 1:3
        2. Naomi's sons marry 1:4
        3. Naomi's sons die: 1:5

II. Return to Bethlehem: 1:6-18

   A. Naomi plans return and tells daughters-in-law to return to their own people: 1:6-9
   B. Their appeal to stay: 1:10
   C. Naomi's answer: 1:11-13
   D. Their response: 1:14
   E. Ruth's declaration: 1:16-18
      1. She does not want to leave Naomi: 1:16
      2. She will go where Naomi goes: 1:16
      3. She will live where Naomi lives: 1:16
      4. Naomi's people shall be hers: 1:16
      5. Naomi's God shall be her God: 1:16
      6. She will remain faithful to death: 1:17

III. Arrival in Bethlehem: 1:19-22

   A. Reception by the city: 1:19
   B. Naomi's response: 1:20-21
   C. The timing of the return: 1:22

IV. Ruth in the fields of Boaz: 2:1-17

   A. Gleaning in the fields: 2:1-3
   B. Boaz's recognition: 2:4-13
   C. Mealtime with Boaz: 2:14
   D. Gleaning the best: 2:15-17
   E. Return from the fields: 2:18-23

V. A special plan: 3:1-18

   A. Naomi's plan: 3:1-5
   B. The results: 3:6-15
   C. The return to Naomi: 3:16-18

VI. The redemption: 4:1-13
   A. The process: 4:1-12
   B. The union of Ruth and Boaz: 4:13-17
   C. The blessing: 4:14-16

VII. The genealogy of David: 4:17-22

SELF-TEST

1. Who was the author of the book of Ruth?

2. State the purpose for the book of Ruth.

3. To whom was the book of Ruth written?

4. State the Life and Ministry Principle of the book of Ruth.

5. Write the Key Verses of Ruth.

(Answers to tests are provided at the conclusion of the final chapter in this manual.)

FOR FURTHER STUDY

1. For further background on the period during which the events of the book of Ruth occurred, refer to the book of Judges.

2. Ruth was one of four women mentioned in the genealogy of Christ in Matthew 1. The others are Tamar Matthew 1:3; Rahab, 1:5; and Bathsheba, 1:6.

3. The obligations of the near kinsman relationship are outlined in Deuteronomy 25:5-10. The property laws with which the unnamed kinsman was concerned are given in Leviticus 25:23.

    The kinsman who was able to redeem had to meet certain requirements:

    -He must be a near kinsman.

    -He must be willing to redeem.

    -He must have the ability to redeem.

    -He must be free himself.

    -He must have the price of redemption.

    Boaz met all of these requirements for Ruth. Jesus met all these requirements as the redeemer of sinful humanity.

4. Study the character of Ruth:

    -Loving, committed: 1:16-17
    -Steadfast: 1:18
    -Humble: 2:2
    -Temperate: 2:14
    -Accountable: 2:18-19
    -Faithful: 2:23
    -Obedient: 3:5
    -Submissive: 3:10
    -Focus on eternal values: 3:10
    -Concerned about appearance of evil: 3:14
    -Patient: 3:18

CHAPTER THIRTEEN

I AND II SAMUEL

OBJECTIVES:

Upon completion of this chapter you will be able to:

- Name the author of the books of I and II Samuel.
- Identify to whom the books were written.
- State the purposes for the books.
- Write the Key Verses of I and II Samuel from memory.
- State the Life and Ministry Principles for the books of I and II Samuel.

I SAMUEL

INTRODUCTION

AUTHOR: Samuel

TO WHOM: Israel

PURPOSE: Continued record of God's dealing with His people.

KEY VERSES: I Samuel 15:22-23

LIFE AND MINISTRY PRINCIPLE: Obedience to God is more important than sacrifice.

MAIN CHARACTERS: Samuel, Elkanah, Hannah, Eli, David, Goliath, Saul, Jonathan, Michal, Abigail

OUTLINE

I. Samuel: The last of the judges: 1:1-7:17

    A. Samuel's birth and childhood: 1:1-2:10
    B. Eli's rejection and Samuel's call: 2:11-3:21
    C. The ark among the Philistines: 4:1-7:1
    D. Samuel's activities as judge: 7:2-17

II. Saul: The first of the kings: 8:1-15:35

    A. Israel's demand for a king: 8:1-22
    B. The choice of Saul: 9:1-11:15
    C. Samuel's farewell address: 12:1-25
    D. Saul's war against the Philistines: 13:1-14:52
    E. Saul's disobedience and rejection: 15:1-35

III. Saul and David: 16:1-31:13

    A. David's anointing and call: 16:1-23
    B. David's victory over Goliath: 17:1-58
    C. David's flight from Saul: 18:1-20:42
    D. David's wanderings: 21:1-30:31
    E. Saul's death: 31:1-13

II SAMUEL

INTRODUCTION

AUTHOR: Samuel

TO WHOM: Israel

PURPOSE: Continue the historical record of God's dealing with His people.

KEY VERSES: II Samuel 7:22-23

LIFE AND MINISTRY PRINCIPLE: God carries out His plan through those obedient to Him in spite of their human frailties.

MAIN CHARACTERS: David, Uriah, Bathsheba, Nathan, Absalom, Abner, Isbosheth, Joab

OUTLINE

I. The triumphs of David: 1:1-10:19

    A. The lament of David over Saul and Jonathan: 1:1-27
    B. David's coronation over Judah: 2:1-7
    C. David establishes national and religious unity: 2:8-6:23
    D. The Davidic covenant: 7:1-29
    E. David's conquests: 8:1-10:19

II. The troubles of David: 11:1-24:25

    A. David's sin and repentance: 11:1-12:31
    B. Amnon and Absalom's crimes: 13:1-18:33
    C. David's restoration to power: 19:1-20:26
    D. The famine and revenge of the Gibeonites: 21:1-14
    E. Heroes in the war with the Philistines: 21:15-22
    F. David's song and last words: 22:1-23:7
    G. David's heroes: 23:8-39
    H. David's census and punishment: 24:1-25

SELF-TEST

1. Who was the author of the books of I and II Samuel?

___

2. State the purpose for the book of I Samuel.

___

3. To whom was the book of I Samuel written?

___

4. State the Life and Ministry Principle of the book of I Samuel.

___

5. Write the Key Verses of I Samuel.

___

6. State the purpose for the book of II Samuel.

___

7. To whom was the book of II Samuel written?

___

8. State the Life and Ministry Principle of the book of II Samuel.

___

9. Write the Key Verses of II Samuel.

___

(Answers to tests are provided at the conclusion of the final chapter in this manual.)

FOR FURTHER STUDY

1. I Samuel records a transition in Israel from a theocracy (where God ruled directly through priests and military leaders) to a monarchy (the rule by various kings).

2. I Samuel 15:22-23 is one of the greatest passages on obedience.

3. I Samuel 16:7 is one of the greatest passages on true human worth.

4. I Samuel 17:4 describes the world's tallest man.

5. I Samuel 18:1 records of one of the most beautiful friendships recorded in the Bible.

6. I Samuel records the first of several conversations of people who had previously left this earth in death. See I Samuel 28; Luke 16:23-31; Revelation 6:9-10 and 7:9-10.

7. Samuel started the first Bible schools recorded in Scripture. These were located at Gilgal, Jericho, and Bethel. See I Samuel 10:10; I Kings 18:13; II Kings 2:3,5; 6:1-2.

8. II Samuel records an important law of sowing and reaping in the spiritual world. After David's prayer of repentance (Psalms 51) God forgave him for adultery and murder (II Samuel 11). But David still harvested sorrow from his actions. The harvest involved the death of an infant son, the rape of a daughter by her own brother, the murder of that brother by another brother, and the rebellion of his favorite son who was later executed by a military commander.

9. Another important principle is taught in II Samuel. It is the principle of doing God's will God's way. It was God's will for David to bring the ark into the Holy City. God's way was for the priests to carry it. At first David did not obey and it resulted in sorrow and death (6:1-7). It is important to harmonize God's will with God's way.

CHAPTER FOURTEEN

I AND II KINGS

OBJECTIVES:

Upon completion of this chapter you will be able to:

- Name the author of the books of I and II Kings.
- Identify to whom these books were written.
- State the purpose for each book.
- Write the Key Verses of the books of I and II Kings from memory.
- State the Life and Ministry Principles for I and II Kings.

I KINGS

INTRODUCTION

AUTHOR: Unknown. Possibly Jeremiah.

TO WHOM: Israel

PURPOSE: Continue the record of God's dealings with His people, Israel.

KEY VERSE: I Kings 19:18

LIFE AND MINISTRY PRINCIPLE: Compromise may seem easy but it is always costly later.

MAIN CHARACTERS: David, Solomon, kings of Judah and Israel (see chart on the kings), Nabath, Ahab, Elijah, Elisha

OUTLINE

I. The reign of King Solomon: 1:1-11:43

    A. His anointing as king: 1:1-53
    B. David's challenge to Solomon and the death of David: 2:1-46
    C. Solomon's marriage and choice of wisdom: 3:1-28
    D. Solomon's administration: 4:1-34

      E.   Building activities of Solomon: 5:1-8:66
      F.   The wealth and splendor of Solomon: 9:1-10:29
      G.   Solomon's sin: 11:1-43

II.   The reigns of the kings of Judah and Israel: 12:1-22:53; also continues into II Kings. (See chart on the kings.)

      A.   Accession of Rehoboam: 12:1-33
      B.   Judah's kings: Rehoboam to Jehoshaphat: 13:1-22:53
      C.   Israel's kings: Jeroboam to Ahaziah: 13:1-22:53
      D.   Ministry of the Prophet Elijah to Israel: 17:1-22:53

II KINGS

INTRODUCTION

AUTHOR: Unknown. Possibly Jeremiah.

TO WHOM: Israel

PURPOSE: Continue the record of God's dealings with His people, Israel.

KEY VERSES: II Kings 2:9-10

LIFE AND MINISTRY PRINCIPLE: Kingdoms of this world are temporal: They rise and fall under God's control.

MAIN CHARACTERS: Kings of Israel and Judah (see chart on the kings), Elisha, Elijah

OUTLINE

I.   Ministry of Elisha and continuing record of the kings of Israel: 1:1-10:36

II.   Record of the kings of Israel and Judah: 11:1-17:41
         Continued from the I Kings record. (See chart of the kings.)

III.   Reigns of Judah's kings: Hezekiah to Zedekiah: 18:1-25:30
         (See chart of the kings.)

SELF-TEST

1. Who was the author of the books of I and II Kings?

   _____

2. State the purpose for the book of I Kings.

   _____

3. To whom was the book of I Kings written?

   _____

4. State the Life and Ministry Principle of the book of I Kings.

   _____

5. Write the Key Verse of I Kings.

   _____

6. State the purpose for the book of II Kings.

   _____

7. To whom was the book of II Kings written?

   _____

8. State the Life and Ministry Principle of the book of II Kings.

   _____

9. Write the Key Verses of II Kings.

   _____

(Answers to tests are provided at the conclusion of the final chapter in this manual.)

FOR FURTHER STUDY

1. I Kings 12 records the disintegration of Israel's 12 tribes. Revelation 7 describes the future uniting of these tribes. The chart in this section summarizes information on the divided kingdoms of Israel and Judah. The map shows the territorial division.

2. King Solomon, a main character in the book of I Kings, wrote Proverbs, Ecclesiastes, and the Song of Solomon. You will study these books later in this course.

3. The following charts of the kings of Israel and Judah will assist you as you study the books of the Kings and Chronicles.

Kings Of Israel

Name Of King	Years of Reign	Dates B.C.	Reference
Jeroboam I	22	976-954	I Kings 11:26-14:20
Nadab	2	954-953	I Kings 15:25-28
Baasha	24	953-930	I Kings 15:27-16:7
Elah	2	930-929	I Kings 16:6-14
Zimri	(7 days)	929	I Kings 16:9-20
Omri	12	929-918	I Kings 16:15-28
Ahab	21	918-898	I Kings 16:28-22:40
Ahaziah	1	898-897	I Kings 22:40-II Kings 1:18
Jehoram	11	897-885	II Kings 3:1-9:25
Jehu	28	885-857	II Kings 9:1-10:36
Jehoahaz	16	857-841	II Kings 13:1-9
Jehoash (Joah)	16	841-825	II Kings 13:10-14:16
Jeroboam II	40	825-773	II Kings 14:23-29
Zechariah	½	773-772	II Kings 14:29-15:12
Shallum	(1 month)	772	II Kings 15:10-15
Menahem	10	772-762	II Kings 15:14-22
Pekahiah	2	762-760	II Kings 15:22-26
Pekah	20	760-730	II Kings 15:27-31
Hoshea	9	730-721	II Kings 15:30-17:6

Kings Of Judah

Name Of King	Years of Reign	Dates B.C.	Reference
Rehoboam	17	976-959	I Kings 11:42-14:31
Abijam	3	959-996	I Kings 14:31-15:8
Asa	41	956-915	I Kings 15:8-24
Jehosaphat	25	915-893	I Kings 22:41-50
Johoram	8	893-886	II Kings 8:16-24
Ahaziah	1	886-885	II Kings 8:24-9:29
Athliah	6	885-879	II Kings 11:1-20
Joash	40	879-840	II Kings 11:1-12:21
Amaziah	29	840-811	II Kings 14:1-20
Azariah (Uzziah)	52	811-759	II Kings 15:1-7
Jotham	18	759-743	II Kings 15:32-38
Ahaz	19	743-727	II Kings 16:1-20
Hezekiah	29	727-698	II Kings 18:1-20:21
Manasseh	55	698-643	II Kings 21:1-18
Amon	2	643-640	II Kings 21:19-26
Josiah	31	640-609	II Kings 22:1-23:30
Jehohaz	(3 months)	609	II Kings 23:31-33
Jehoiakim	11	609-597	II Kings 23:34-24:5
Jehoiachin	(3 months)	597	II Kings 24:6-16
Zedekiah	11	597-586	II Kings 24:17-25:30

Summary Chart Of The Divided Kingdom

ISRAEL 933-722 B.C.	JUDAH 933-586 B.C.
Other names:	Other Names:
The Ten Tribes The Northern Kingdom Samaria/Ephraim	The Two Tribes The Southern Kingdom House Of David
Ruling Families:	Ruling Families:
Nine dynasties or ruling families Nineteen kings (all wicked)	One dynasty (David) Twenty kings (Many Good)
One Suicide/Seven assassinations	Five assassinations
Duration:	Duration:
211 years	347 years
Captivity:	Captivity:
Punished by captivity to Assyria Dispersed among nations	Carried to Babylon Returned after 70 years Rebuilt Jerusalem and temple
Did not regain freedom	
Territory:	Territory:
More than 2/3 of Canaan The best portion	Less than 1/3 of Canaan The temple and Jerusalem
Religion:	Religion:
Forsook God-ordained way of worship Worshiped golden calf all through history Added Baal and Asherah worship during Ahab's reign	Idolatry added to worship Frequent reforms God-fearing kings

CHAPTER FIFTEEN

I AND II CHRONICLES

OBJECTIVES:

Upon completion of this chapter you will be able to:

- Name the author of the book of I and II Chronicles.
- Identify to whom these books were written.
- State the purpose for each book.
- Write the Key Verses of the books of I and II Chronicles from memory.
- State the Life and Ministry Principles for I and II Chronicles.

I CHRONICLES

INTRODUCTION

AUTHOR: Unknown. Possibly Ezra.

TO WHOM: Israel

PURPOSE: Record of the religious history of Judah.

KEY VERSE: I Chronicles 29:11

LIFE AND MINISTRY PRINCIPLE: When God is exalted His people are blessed.

MAIN CHARACTERS: King David, Solomon

OUTLINE

I. Genealogies from Adam to David: 1:1-9:44

    A. From Adam to Jacob: 1:1-2:2
    B. From Jacob to David: 2:2-9:44

II. History of King David: 10:1-29:30

    A. The death of King Saul: 10:1-14
    B. Capture of Zion and David's heroes: 11:1-12:40
    C. David's prosperous reign: 13:1-22:1
    D. David's religious accomplishments: 22:2-29:30

II CHRONICLES

INTRODUCTION

AUTHOR: Unknown. Possibly Ezra.

TO WHOM: Israel

PURPOSE: Record of the religious history of Judah.

KEY VERSE: 2 Chronicles 7:14

LIFE AND MINISTRY PRINCIPLE: God's blessing comes through humbling ourselves and seeking Him.

MAIN CHARACTERS: King Solomon and his successors from Rehoboam to Zedekiah. (See chart of the kings of Judah.)

OUTLINE

I. History of King Solomon: 1:1-9:31

    A. Solomon's wealth and wisdom: 1:1-17
    B. Solomon's building and dedication of the temple: 2:1-7:22
    C. Solomon's various activities: 8:1-9:28
    D. Solomon's death: 9:29-31

II. History of the kings of Judah: 10:1-36:23

    A. Kings from Rehoboam to Zedekiah: 10:1-36:21

    (For detailed study of these kings, see the chart of the kings of Judah in the preceding chapter.)

    B. The edict of Cyrus: 36:22-23

SELF-TEST

1. Who was the author of the books of I and II Chronicles?

   _____

2. State the purpose for the book of I Chronicles.

   _____

3. To whom was the book of I Chronicles written?

   _____

4. State the Life and Ministry Principle of the book of I Chronicles.

   _____

5. Write the Key Verse of I Chronicles.

   _____

6. State the purpose for the book of II Chronicles.

   _____

7. To whom was the book of II Chronicles written?

   _____

8. State the Life and Ministry Principle of the book of II Chronicles.

   _____

9. Write the Key Verse of II Chronicles.

   _____

(Answers to tests are provided at the conclusion of the final chapter in this manual.)

FOR FURTHER STUDY

1. Although there is much similar material in the books of II Samuel, the Kings, and the Chronicles, each book is written to accomplish a specific purpose.

    For example, II Samuel and I and II Kings present the political history of both Israel and Judah. In I and II Chronicles a detailed religious history of Judah only is presented.

    II Samuel and I and II Kings focus on the rulers and prophets of the period. I and II Chronicles focus on the priests and the temple.

    As you study these books in detail, look for the differing emphasis of the material which is repeated.

2. II Chronicles is a book of revivals. Great revivals occurred under:

    - Asa: II Chronicles 15
    - Jehosaphat: II Chronicles 20
    - Joash: II Chronicles 23-24
    - Hezekiah: II Chronicles 29-31
    - Josiah: II Chronicles 35

3. Key words in Chronicles to mark in your Bible:

    - house
    - ark
    - covenant
    - cry (cried)
    - seek (sought)
    - heart
    - pray (prayer, prayed)
    - prophet(s)

4. Many lessons about prayer and seeking God can be learned from these books. Review what you learn from marking the key words. Study especially 2 Chronicles 6.

5. What did you learn from the successes and failures of men such as Jehosaphat, Hezekiah, and Uzziah?

CHAPTER SIXTEEN

EZRA

OBJECTIVES:

Upon completion of this chapter you will be able to:

- Name the author of the book of Ezra.
- Identify to whom the book of Ezra was written.
- State the purpose for the book of Ezra.
- Write the Key Verse of the book of Ezra from memory.
- State the Life and Ministry Principle for the book of Ezra.

INTRODUCTION

AUTHOR: Ezra

TO WHOM: Israel

PURPOSE: Records the return of Israel from exile and rebuilding of the Jerusalem temple.

KEY VERSE: Ezra 6:16

LIFE AND MINISTRY PRINCIPLE: Return and restoration are basic principles of repentance.

MAIN CHARACTERS: Ezra, Jeshua, Zerubbabel, Cyrus, Haggai, Zechariah, Artaxerxes

OUTLINE

I. Restoration under Zerubbabel: 1:1-6:22

    A. First return of exiles: 1:1-2:70
        1. Edict of Cyrus: 1:1-11
            (a) The writing of the edict: 1:2-4
            (b) The desire of the people: 1:5-11
        2. List of exiles: 2:1-70
    B. Restoration of public worship : 3:1-6:22
        1. Rebuilding of temple: 3:1-6:15

          (a)   Worship reinstated in Jerusalem: 3:1-7
          (b)   Work on the temple: 3:8-13
          (c)   Satan tries to hinder the work: 4:1-24
          (d)   The prophets come to help: 5:1-2
          (e)   The governor's questions: 5:3-5
          (f)   The letter to Darius: 5:6-17
          (g)   The search: 6:1-12
          (h)   Tatnai's response: 6:13-15
      2.   Dedication of temple: 6:16-22

II.   Reforms under Ezra: 7:1-10:44

    A.   Second Return of Exiles 7:1-8:36
        1.   Ezra's background and preparation: 7:1-10
        2.   The letter of Artaxerxes: 7:11-26
        3.   The response of Ezra: 7:27-28
    B.   Correction of social evils: 9:1-10:44
        1.   God's people compromising: 9:1-2
        2.   Ezra's supplication: 9:3-15
        3.   Conviction settles on the people: 10:1-8
        4.   Confession and repentance: 10:9-16
        5.   The list of offenders: 10:18-44

SELF-TEST

1. Who was the author of the book of Ezra?

   _____

2. State the purpose for the book of Ezra.

   _____

   _____

   _____

3. To whom was the book of Ezra written?

   _____

   _____

4. State the Life and Ministry Principle of the book of Ezra.

   _____

   _____

   _____

5. Write the Key Verse of Ezra.

   _____

   _____

   _____

(Answers to tests are provided at the conclusion of the final chapter in this manual.)

FOR FURTHER STUDY

1. Read Psalms 137. This chapter records the sorrow of God's people as they made the trip from Jerusalem to captivity in Babylon. Read Psalms 126 which describes the joy of the return to Jerusalem from captivity.

2. The divided kingdoms of Israel and Judah were both taken captive by enemies. Israel was taken captive by Assyria in 721 B.C. Judah was taken captive by Babylon in 606 B.C. The return of God's people to Jerusalem from captivity was as follows:

    536 B.C. Zerubbabel with 42,360 Jews, 7,337 servants, 200 singers, 736 horses, 245 mules, 435 camels, 6,720 asses, and 5,400 gold and silver vessels.

    457 B.C. Ezra with 1,754 men, 100 talents of gold, 750 talents of silver. It is not stated whether women and children were in this group of returning exiles.

    444 B.C. Nehemiah, with an army escort, to rebuild and fortify Jerusalem.

3. There were three trips into Babylonian bondage. In Ezra, there are three journeys back to the Promised Land.

    Three trips into Babylon:

    -In the days of Daniel: 606 B.C.
    -In the days of Ezekiel: 597 B.C.
    -In the days of King Zedekiah: 586 B.C.
    Three trips into freedom:

    -Led by Zerubbabel and Joshua: 538 B.C.
    -Led by Ezra: 456 B.C.
    -Led by Nehemiah: 446 B.C.

CHAPTER SEVENTEEN

NEHEMIAH

OBJECTIVES:

Upon completion of this chapter you will be able to:

- Name the author of the book of Nehemiah.
- Identify to whom the book of Nehemiah was written.
- State the purpose for the book of Nehemiah.
- Write the Key Verse of the book of Nehemiah from memory.
- State the Life and Ministry Principle for the book of Nehemiah.

INTRODUCTION

AUTHOR: Nehemiah

TO WHOM: Israel

PURPOSE: Continuation of the history of Israel. Record of the rebuilding of the walls of Jerusalem.

KEY VERSE: Nehemiah 6:3

LIFE AND MINISTRY PRINCIPLE: There is no opportunity without opposition. Faith without works is dead.

MAIN CHARACTERS: Nehemiah, Sanballat, Geshem, Gashmu, Shemiah, Tobiah, Hananiah, Ezra, Artaxerxes

OUTLINE

I. Introduction: 1:1-11

    A. Bad news from Jerusalem: 1:1-3
    B. Nehemiah's response: 1:4-11

II. Preparation for the task: 2:1-20

    A. With the King: 2:1-8
    B. With the governors: 2:9-10
    C. In Jerusalem: 2:11-15
    D. With the leaders of the people: 2:15-20

III. Restoration of the walls: 3:1-6:19

    A. List of builders and organization: 3:1-32
    B. External and internal opposition: 4-6:14
        1. External opposition:
            (a) Direct criticism: 2:19
            (b) Mocking and scorn: 4:1-3
            (c) False accusations: 6:5-7
            (d) Strikes at times of vulnerability: 4:6
            (e) Diversion: 6:2
            (f) Popular influence: 6:2
            (g) Threats, fear: 6:5-9
            (h) Compromise: 5:14-19
            (i) Fighting, hindering: 4:8
            (j) Conspiracy: 4:8; 6:2
            (k) Threats and fear: 6:5-9
        2. Internal opposition:
            (a) Discouragement: 4:10-11
            (b) Dissension: 5:1-19
            (c) Weak believers: 4:12
            (d) Opposition of religious leaders: 3:5
            (e) False prophets of God: 6:10-13
    C. The wall is finished: 6:15-19

IV. Control and census: 7:1-73

    A. City controls established: 7:1-4
    B. Census of returning exiles: 7:5-73

V. Religious reforms by Ezra and Nehemiah: 8:1-13:31

    A. Reading of the law: 8:1-8:18
    B. Confession and prayer: 9:1-37
    C. Renewal of the covenant: 9:38-10:39
    D. List of residents: 11:1-12:26
    E. Dedication of the wall: 12:27-47

F.   Reforms of Nehemiah: 13:1-31

Inspirational Slogans

Nehemiah's ten inspirational slogans:

-The good hand of my God upon me: 2:8
-Let us rise up and build: 2:18
-The God of Heaven will prosper us: 2:20
-The people had a mind to work: 4:6
-Remember the Lord and fight: 4:14
-God shall fight for us: 4:20
-O God, strengthen my hands: 6:9
-This work was wrought of our God: 6:16
-The joy of the Lord is our strength: 8:10
-Remember, O My God: 13:29,31

SELF-TEST

1. Who was the author of the book of Nehemiah?

   _____

2. State the purpose for the book of Nehemiah.

   _____

   _____

   _____

3. To whom was the book of Nehemiah written?

   _____

   _____

4. State the Life and Ministry Principle of the book of Nehemiah.

   _____

   _____

   _____

5. Write the Key Verse of Nehemiah.

   _____

   _____

   _____

(Answers to tests are provided at the conclusion of the final chapter in this manual.)

FOR FURTHER STUDY

1. A work for God will always be met by human and Satanic opposition both internal and external. As you study the book of Nehemiah, make a list of the various attacks of the enemy designed to stop the work of God.

2. The gates in the wall around Jerusalem are a type of the Christian life. That means although they were actual gates, they were also symbols of spiritual truth:

Name Of Gate	Symbolizes	References Nehemiah	Other
Sheep gate	The cross	3:1	John 10:11
Fish gate	Soul-winning	3:3	Matthew 4:19
Old gate	Old nature	3:6	Romans 6:1-23
Valley gate	Suffering and testing	3:13	II Corinthians 1:3-5
Dung gate	Works of the flesh	3:14	Galatians 5:16-21
Fountain gate	Holy Spirit	3:15	John 7:37-39
Water gate	Word of God	3:26	John 4:10-14
Horse gate	Believer's warfare	3:28	Ephesians 6:10-17
Eastern gate	Return of Jesus	3:29	Ezekiel 43:1,2
Miphkad gate	Judgment seat of Jesus	3:31	I Corinthians 3:9-15; II Corinthians 5:10

CHAPTER EIGHTEEN

ESTHER

OBJECTIVES:

Upon completion of this chapter you will be able to:

- Name the author of the book of Esther.
- Identify to whom the book of Esther was written.
- State the purpose for the book of Esther.
- Write the Key Verse of the book of Esther from memory.
- State the Life and Ministry Principle for the book of Esther.

INTRODUCTION

AUTHOR: Unknown

TO WHOM: The Jews scattered throughout Persia.

PURPOSE: Continuation of history of Israel. Also to recount the providential care of God for His people.

KEY VERSE: Esther 4:14

LIFE AND MINISTRY PRINCIPLE: God meets the crises of life with human vessels which He has prepared.

MAIN CHARACTERS: Esther, Vashti, Haman, Mordecai, Ahasuerus

OUTLINE

I. Introduction: 1:1-22

    A. The great feasts: 1:1-9
    B. A domestic problem: 1:10-12
    C. A royal commandment: 1:13-22

II. A new queen: 2:1-21

    A. The search for a queen: 2:1-4
    B. Esther enters the competition: 2:5-11
        1. Mordecai's background: 2:5-6
        2. Esther's background: 2:7
    C. Esther in the custody of Hegai: 2:8-11
    D. The women presented before the king: 2:12-14
    E. Esther selected as queen: 2:15-17
    F. The feast for Esther: 2:18
    G. Esther's secret: 2:19

III. Two men, two plots: 2:21-3:15

    A. The plot overthrown by Mordecai: 2:22-23
        1. Mordecai in the king's gate: 2:22-23
        2. Mordecai aborts the plot: 2:21-22
        3. The two criminals hanged: 2:23
    B. The promotion and plot of Haman: 3:1-15
        1. Haman promoted above all other princes: 3:1
        2. The problem between Haman and Mordecai: 3:2-6
        3. Haman's vengeful plot: 3:7-15

IV. Despair and deliverance: 4:1-7:10

    A. Despair of the Jews: 4:1-3
    B. Despair of the Queen: 4:4-9
    C. A plan for deliverance: 4:10-5:14
        1. The plan: 4:10-17
        2. Before the King: 5:1-3
        3. Invitation to a banquet: 5:4-8
        4. Haman's pride: 5:9-14
    D. Mordecai honored: 6:1-14
        1. The king's reading: 6:1-3
        2. Haman sought for advice: 6:4-5
        3. Haman prideful response: 6:6-9
        4. Haman's mortification as Mordecai is honored: 6:10-12
        5. The response of Haman's family and friends: 6:13-14
    E. The feast of Esther: 7:1-6
    F. Haman punished: 7:7-10

V. The new kingdom order: 8:1-10:3

    A. New orders from the king: 8:1-14
    B. Mordecai honored: 8:15-17
    C. Deliverance of the Jews: 9:1-11
    D. House of Haman destroyed: 9:12-14
    E. The feast of Purim: 9:15-32
    F. Representation by Mordecai: 10:1-3

SELF-TEST

1. Who was the author of the book of Esther?

2. State the purpose for the book of Esther.

3. To whom was the book of Esther written?

4. State the Life and Ministry Principle of the book of Esther.

5. Write the Key Verse of Esther.

(Answers to tests are provided at the conclusion of the final chapter in this manual.)

FOR FURTHER STUDY

1. The longest verse in the Bible is Esther 8:9. It contains 90 words in the English King James version.

2. Note the contrasts between the books of Ruth and Esther:

    -Ruth was a Gentile who lived among Jews.
    -Esther was a Jew who lived among Gentiles.
    -Ruth married a Jew.
    -Esther married a Gentile.

    The outcome of both stories was determined through a midnight meeting:

    -Ruth talked with Boaz: Ruth 3:8-13
    -Haman talked with the king: Esther 6:1-10

3. Study Haman as a type of Satan:

    -Above all princes: 3:1
    -Full of wrath: 3:5
    -Full of scorn: 3:6
    -Destroyer: 3:6
    -Enemy: 3:10
    -Materialistic: 3:8,9,11; 4:7
    -Perplexes: 3:15
    -Taxes prey: 3:13
    -None escape: 4:13
    -Man of indignation: 5:9
    -Proud: 5:11-12; 6:6-9
    -Petty: 5:13; 6:12
    -Plotter: 3:1-15; 5:14; 6:4
    -Adversary and enemy: 7:6
    -Immoral: 7:8
    -Wicked devises: 9:25
    -Fears before the King: 7:6
    -Falls before the people of God: 6:13

AN INTRODUCTION TO THE BOOKS OF POETRY

The five books of poetry show a progression of spiritual life.

Job: Describes the death to the old life of self.

Psalms: Illustrates the new life in God, expressing itself in praise, prayer, adoration, supplication, confession, and intercession. Psalms is the hymn book and worship manual of the Bible.

Proverbs: Gives heavenly, yet practical, wisdom for life on earth.

Ecclesiastes: Tells of the vanity of pursuing life "under the sun" apart from God.

Song of Solomon: Provides an example of life with meaning by a personal relationship with Jesus Christ. Biblical poetry is different from most types of poetry because it is written in Hebrew poetic structure. Keys to understanding this structure are given in the Harvestime International Institute Course entitled "*Creative Bible Study Methods.*"

CHAPTER NINETEEN

JOB

OBJECTIVES:

Upon completion of this chapter you will be able to:

- Name the author of the book of Job.
- Identify to whom the book of Job was written.
- State the purpose for the book of Job.
- Write the Key Verses of the book of Job from memory.
- State the Life and Ministry Principle for the book of Job.

INTRODUCTION

AUTHOR: Unknown

TO WHOM: The book is not specifically addressed to anyone but is applicable to all believers who experience suffering.

PURPOSE: This book wrestles with the question, "Why do the righteous suffer?"

KEY VERSES: Job 19:25-27; 23:10

LIFE AND MINISTRY PRINCIPLE: There is a spiritual reason behind suffering of the righteous. Suffering is not necessarily evidence of God's displeasure.

MAIN CHARACTERS: God, Satan, Job, Job's wife, and his friends, Eliphaz, Bildad, Zophar, and Elihu.

OUTLINE

I. Prologue: 1:1-2:13

    A. Introduction: 1:1-5
    B. Satan's first appearance and accusation: 1:6-12
    C. Job's trial: 1:13-22
    D. Satan's second appearance and accusation: 2:1-6
    E. Job's trial: 2:7-13

II. First cycle of speeches: 3:1-14:22

    A. Job's speech: 3:1-26
    B. Eliphaz's speech: 4:1-5:27
    C. Job's reply: 6:1-7:21
    D. Bildad's speech: 8:1-22
    E. Job's reply: 9:1-10:22
    F. Zophar's speech: 11:1-20
    G. Job's reply: 12:1-14:22

III. Second cycle of speeches: 15:1-21:34

    A. Eliphaz's speech: 15:1-35
    B. Job's reply: 16:1-17:16
    C. Bildad's speech: 18:1-21
    D. Job's reply: 19:1-29
    E. Zophar's speech: 20:1-29
    F. Job's reply: 21:1-34

IV. Third cycle of speeches: 32:1-37

    A. Eliphaz's final speech: 22:1-30
    B. Job's reply: 23:1-24:25
    C. Bildad's final speech: 25:1-6
    D. Job's reply: 26:1-31:40

V. Elihu's speeches: 32:1-37:24

    A. First speech: 32:1-33:33
    B. Second speech: 34:1-37
    C. Third speech: 35:1-16
    D. Fourth speech 36:1-37:24

VI. God's answer: 38:1-42:6

    A. First speech: 38:1-40:5
        1. God questions Job from the realm of creation: 38:1-38
        2. God questions Job from the realm of animals: 38:39-39:30
        3. God demands an answer to His questions: 40:1-2
        4. Job's first answer to God: 40:3-5
    B. Second speech: 40:6-42:6
        1. God tells Job to save himself: 40:6-14

       2.   God compares the power of Job with Behemoth: 40:15-24
       3.   God compares the power of Job with Leviathan: 41:1-34
       4.   Job's second answer to God: 42-1-6
            a.   He confesses lack of understanding: 42:1-3
            b.   He repents of His rebellion: 42:4-6

VII.   Epilogue: 42:1-17

     A.   Divine rebuke of Job's three friends: 42:1-9
     B.   Job's restoration: 42:10-17

SELF-TEST

1. Who was the author of the book of Job?

   _____

2. State the purpose for the book of Job.

   _____

   _____

   _____

3. To whom was the book of Job written?

   _____

   _____

4. State the Life and Ministry Principle of the book of Job.

   _____

   _____

   _____

5. Write the Key Verses of Job.

   _____

   _____

   _____

   _____

(Answers to tests are provided at the conclusion of the final chapter of this manual.)

FOR FURTHER STUDY

1. List the name of each character who speaks in the book of Job. Summarize the thoughts presented by each. The answers for the problem of suffering is dealt with from different perspectives by the friends of Job. They all agree that Job must have sinned.

    Eliphaz views the problem from the perspective of philosophy.

    Bildad bases his advice on tradition rooted in history.

    Zophar bases his ideas on assumption and is the voice of orthodox morality.

    Elihu was an intellectual and bases his advice on education and logic.

2. Compare Job 1:21 with Philippians 4:11-12

3. The book of Job provides the most extended description of the world's history before man. See chapters 38-39. Other statements about the earth reveal it is suspended in space (26:7) and that it is a sphere shape (22:14).

4. The book of Job reveals two important truths:

    First, there is a spiritual reason behind the suffering of the righteous: Job 1:6-12; 2:1-6.

    Second, Satan cannot afflict a believer without the permission of God: Job 1:6-12; 2:1-6. God knows how much we can bear and will not let Satan go beyond this point (I Corinthians 10:13).

5. The book reveals several reasons for Job's suffering:

    -That Satan might be silenced: 1:9-11; 2:4,5
    -That Job might see himself as he really was: 40:4; 42:6
    -That Job might see God: 42:5
    -That Job's friends might learn not to judge: 42:7
    -That Job might learn to pray for his critics rather than lash out against them verbally: 42:10
    -To show that God's plans for His children eventually result in happiness: 42:10

CHAPTER TWENTY

PSALMS

OBJECTIVES:

Upon completion of this chapter you will be able to:

- Name the author of the book of Psalms.
- Identify to whom the book of Psalms was written.
- State the purpose for the book of Psalms.
- Write, from memory, the Key Verse of the book of Psalms.
- State the Life and Ministry Principle for the book of Psalms.

INTRODUCTION

AUTHOR: All the Psalms were written by King David with the exception of the following:

-Asaph: 50; 73-83
-Heman: 88
-Ethan: 89
-Solomon: 127
-Moses: 90
-Hezekiah: 120, 121,123,125, 126, 128-130, 132, 134
-Author Unknown: 1, 10, 33, 43, 66, 67, 71, 911-94, 96-100, 102, 104, 106, 107, 111-119, 135, 136, 137, 146-150

TO WHOM: Israel, but the book has been used for devotion, prayer, and praise by believers down through the centuries.

PURPOSE: The book of Psalms was known as the hymn book of Israel. The word "Psalms" means "songs to the accompaniment of a stringed instrument." It is the prayer and praise book of the Bible.

KEY VERSE: Psalm 95:1

LIFE AND MINISTRY PRINCIPLE: Prayer, praise, intercession, and confession are all part of true worship.

MAIN CHARACTERS: There are several people mentioned in Psalms, either in the Psalm itself or in the title of the Psalm:

-Abimelech (Achish): I Samuel 21:10-15
-Absalom: I Samuel 13
-Ahimelech: I Samuel 22:9-19
-Aram-naharaim: Armeans of northwest Mesopotamia
-Aram-zobath: Armeans of central Syria
-Asaph: Levite, family of singers: II Chronicles 5:12
-Bath-sheba: II Samuel ll
-Cush the Benjamite (Shimel): II Samuel 16:5-14
-Doeg the Edomite: I Samuel 22:9-23
-Ethan the Ezrahite (A wise man in Solomon's time): I Kings 4:31
-Heman the Ezrahite (Levite family of singers): II Chronicles 5:12
-Jeduthun (Chief musician in the temple): I Chronicles 16:41-42
-Korah (Levite, head of the temple musicians):I Chronicles 6:22
-Nathan (Prophet of God): II Samuel 12:1-14
-Sons of Korah (Musical Levite family): I Chronicles 6:22
-Ziphites: I Samuel 23:19

OUTLINE

It is difficult to outline the book of Psalms as each chapter focuses on different subject matter. Many of the Psalms have titles which either tell the occasion when the Psalm was written or the purpose of the Psalm. Some of the Psalms were not given titles so we can only speculate as to when and why they were written. The Harvestime International Institute course entitled *"Creative Bible Study Methods"* provides a special study form for outlining each chapter in Psalms. The general outline of this book consists of five major divisions:

Part One: Psalms l-41

Number of Psalms:	41
Summary of content:	Concerns man, his state of blessedness, fall, and recovery.
Key word:	Man
Final doxology:	41:13

Part Two: Psalms 42-72

Number of Psalms:	31
Summary of content:	Israel, her ruin, her Redeemer
Key word:	Deliverance
Final doxology:	42:18-19

Part Three: Psalms 73-89

Number of Psalms:	17
Summary of content:	The sanctuary, looking forward to its establishment.
Key word:	Sanctuary
Final doxology:	89:52

Part Four: Psalms 90-106

Number of Psalms:	17
Summary of content:	The earth: The blessing needed, anticipated, and enjoyed.
Key words:	Unrest, wandering (which describes the believer's position in the present world)
Final doxology:	106:48

Part Five: Psalms 107-150

Number of Psalms:	44
Summary of content:	The Word of God
Key words:	Word of God
Final doxology:	150:6

SELF-TEST

1. Who was the author of the book of Psalms?

   _____

   _____

2. State the purpose for the book of Psalms.

   _____

   _____

   _____

3. To whom was the book of Psalms written?

   _____

   _____

4. State the Life and Ministry Principle of the book of Psalms.

   _____

   _____

5. Write the Key Verse of Psalms.

   _____

   _____

   _____

(Answers to tests are provided at the conclusion of the final chapter of this manual.)

FOR FURTHER STUDY

INSTRUMENTS MENTIONED IN PSALMS:

-Alamoth: High-pitched harps
-Gittith: Similar to the modern guitar
-Mahalath: Flutes
-Mahalath Leannoth: Special flutes played in times of mourning
-Sheminith: A lyre or five stringed harp

TYPES OF PSALMS:

Psalms Of Instruction: The word "Maschil" in the title means these and other Psalms are to be used for instruction or teaching. (Psalms 32, 44, 52, and 78 are examples.)

Psalms Of Adoration: In these Psalms God's greatness, mercy, love, and power are the theme. (See Psalms 8, 29.)

Psalms Of History: These recall historical events of the nation of Israel. (See Psalms 78, 105 and 106.)

Psalms Of Supplication: Making requests of God. (An example is Psalm 86.)

Psalms Of Thanksgiving: An example is Psalm 18.

Imprecatory Psalms: The word "imprecatory" means cursing. These Psalms are not for personal revenge nor is bad language used. As a prophet of God, the writer speaks out against sin and the enemies of God. (Examples of these are Psalms 35, 55, 58, 59, 69, 83, 109, 137 and 140.)

Confession Psalms: Examples are Psalms 6, 32, 38, 51, 102, 130 and 143.

Messianic Psalms: These Psalms, or portions of them, give prophecies relating to the coming of the Messiah, Jesus Christ. They are recorded on the next page to enable your further study.

Prophecies Concerning Jesus In The Book Of Psalms

Psalm	New Testament Fulfillment
8:3-8	Hebrews 2:5-10; I Corinthians 15:27
72:6-17	This will be fulfilled in the future
89:3-4,26, 28-29,34-37	Acts 2:30
109:6-19	Acts 1:16-20
132:12b	Acts 2:30
45:6-7	Hebrews 1:8-9
102:25-27	Hebrews 1:10-12
110:1-7	Matthew 22:43-45; Acts 2:33-35; Hebrews 1:13; 5:6-10; 6:20,7-24
2:1-12	Acts 4:25-28; 13:33; Hebrews 1:5; 5:5
16:10	Acts 2:24-31; 13:35-37
22:1-31	Matthew 27:35-46; John 19:23-25; Hebrews 2:12
40:6-8	Hebrews 10:5-10
69:25	Acts 1:16-20

CHAPTER TWENTY-ONE

PROVERBS

OBJECTIVES:

Upon completion of this chapter you will be able to:

- Name the author of the book of Proverbs.
- Identify to whom the book of Proverbs was written.
- State the purpose for the book of Proverbs.
- Write the Key Verse of the book of Proverbs from memory.
- State the Life and Ministry Principle for the book of Proverbs.

INTRODUCTION

AUTHOR: Solomon, the son of King David, wrote most of the Proverbs. It is recorded in I Kings 4:32 that Solomon spoke three thousand proverbs under the inspiration of God. Some of these are preserved for us by the Holy Spirit in the book of Proverbs. Two chapters in Proverbs are written by authors with another name: Agur wrote chapter 30 and Lemuel wrote chapter 31. Some of the Proverbs Solomon set in order himself. This means he not only wrote them but also arranged them in the order in which they are presented in the Bible. Other Proverbs of Solomon were put in their order by King Hezekiah's men

TO WHOM: Israel, but the truths for practical living are applicable to all believers.

PURPOSE: The purposes of this book are given in Proverbs 1:1-6. Read them in your Bible. An introduction to Proverbs is given in Ecclesiastes 12:8-14. Read this passage in your Bible.

KEY VERSE: Proverbs 3:13

LIFE AND MINISTRY PRINCIPLE: Vertical wisdom is necessary for horizontal living. Proverbs is a collection of wise principles given by God to man (vertical) to govern living with others (horizontal).

MAIN CHARACTERS: The authors, Solomon, King Lemuel, and Agur. The woman apart from God is called the "strange woman." The final chapter of Proverbs presents a contrast to her by describing the "virtuous woman" who knows God.

OUTLINE

The word "proverbs" means "a brief saying instead of many words." Each verse in Proverbs is a concise summary of an important truth. It is difficult to make a general outline of the book because each chapter and sometimes each verse within the chapter deals with a different subject. The reason for writing these brief sayings or "proverbs" is to condense wisdom to help us remember spiritual truths better. The Proverbs are short summaries of great spiritual truths. Here is a general outline of the book:

I. Introduction: 1:1-6

II. Lessons on wisdom: 1:7-9:18

    A. The call of wisdom: 1:7-33
    B. The rewards of wisdom: 2:1-7:27
    C. Praise of divine wisdom: 8:1-9:18

III. Miscellaneous proverbs of Solomon set in order himself: 10:1-22:16

(From this chapter through chapter 25 are various observations about Christian virtues and their opposite sinful attitudes and responses.)

IV. Collections of proverbs of wise men: 22:17-24:34

V. Proverbs of Solomon set in order by Hezekiah's scribes: 25:1-29:27

    A. Observations about kings; quarrels; relationships with others: 25:1-28
    B. Comments on fools, sluggards, and busybodies: 26:1-28
    C. Self-love, true love; offenses; thoughts on household care: 27:1-27
    D. Contrasts of the wicked and righteous: 28:1-28
    E. Proverbs about public government and private affairs: 29:1-27

VI. A proverb of Agur: Confessions and instructions: 30:1-33

VII. A proverb of Lemuel: A lesson in chastity and temperance; praise of a good wife: 31:1-31

SELF-TEST

1. Who was the author of the book of Proverbs?

2. State the purpose for the book of Proverbs.

3. To whom was the book of Proverbs written?

4. State the Life and Ministry Principle of the book of Proverbs.

5. Write the Key Verse of Proverbs.

(Answers to tests are provided at the conclusion of the final chapter in this manual.)

FOR FURTHER STUDY

1. Key words to study in Proverbs include:

    -wisdom
    -knowledge
    -instruction
    -folly
    -fear, fear of the Lord
    -life
    -law (commandments) righteousness/evil/justice
    -my son

2. Study the following groups mentioned in Proverbs:

    -Seven things God hates: 6:16-19
    -Two things the author requests of God: 30:7-9
    -Four things which are never satisfied: 30:15-16
    -Four things which the earth finds unbearable: 30:21-23
    -Four wonderful things: 30:18-19
    -Four small but wise things: 30:24-28
    -Four stately rulers: 30:29-31

3. Study the different fools mentioned in Proverbs:

    -The simple fool: 1:4,22; 7:7; 21:11
    -The hardened fool: 1:7; 10:23; 12:23; 17:10; 20:3; 27:22
    -The arrogant fool: 3:34; 21:24; 22:10; 29:8
    -The brutish fool: 17:21; 26:3; 30:22

4. Record what the book of Proverbs teaches on the following subjects:

-A good name	-Self control	-Masters/servants
-Youth and discipline	-Strong drink	-Anger/strife
-Business matters	-Friendship	-Rich/poor, poverty/wealth
-Marriage	-Words/tongue	-Women
-Immorality	-Wisdom and folly	-Oppression
-Evil companions	-Laziness/work	-Scorners
-Wisdom	-Proud/humble	

CHAPTER TWENTY-TWO

ECCLESIASTES

OBJECTIVES:

Upon completion of this chapter you will be able to:

- Name the author of the book of Ecclesiastes.
- Identify to whom the book of Ecclesiastes was written.
- State the purpose for the book of Ecclesiastes.
- Write the Key Verse of the book of Ecclesiastes from memory.
- State the Life and Ministry Principle for the book of Ecclesiastes.

INTRODUCTION

AUTHOR: Solomon

TO WHOM: Israel and believers in general with a special emphasis towards youth.

PURPOSE: A description of the quest for life apart from God.

KEY VERSE: Ecclesiastes 12:13

LIFE AND MINISTRY PRINCIPLE: Life apart from God is futile.

MAIN CHARACTERS: Solomon. No other characters are mentioned by name.

OUTLINE

I. Searching by personal experimenting: 1:1-2:26

    A. By wisdom: 1:12-18
    B. By pleasure: 2:1-11
    C. A comparison of the two: 2:12-23
    D. The first tentative conclusion: 2:24-26

II. Searching by general observation: 3:1-5:20

    A. Of natural order: 3:1-22
    B. Of human society: 4:1-16
    C. His advice in view of these two: 5:1-17
        1. Regarding religion: 5:1-7
        2. Regarding society: 5:8
        3. Regarding riches: 5:9-17
    D. The third tentative conclusion: 5:18-20

III. Searching by practical morality: 6:1-8:17

    A. Economic level: 6:1-12
    B. Reputation: 7:1-22
    C. Education: 7:23-8:1
    D. Social position: 8:2-14
    E. The third tentative conclusion 8:15-17

IV. The search reviewed: 9:1-12:12

Solomon concludes the following about life apart from God (references relate back to his discussion of these facts):

    A. It is utterly futile: 2:11
    B. It is filled with repetition: 3:1-8
    C. It is filled with sorrow: 4:1
    D. It is grievous and frustrating: 2:17
    E. It is uncertain: 9:11-12
    F. It is without purpose: 4:2,3; 8:15
    G. It is incurable: 1:15
    H. It is unjust: 7:15; 8:14; 9:11; 10:6-7
    I. It is on the level of animal existence: 3:19

V. The search concluded; A final conclusion: 12:13-14

    A. What we should do: 12:13
        1. Fear God: 12:13
        2. Keep His commandments: 12:13
    B. Why we should do it: 12:13b-14
        1. It is the whole duty of man: 12:13b
        2. We will someday be judged: 12:14

SELF-TEST

1. Who was the author of the book of Ecclesiastes?

   _____

2. State the purpose for the book of Ecclesiastes.

   _____

   _____

   _____

3. To whom was the book of Ecclesiastes written?

   _____

   _____

4. State the Life and Ministry Principle of the book of Ecclesiastes.

   _____

   _____

   _____

5. Write the Key Verse of Ecclesiastes.

   _____

   _____

   _____

(Answers to tests are provided at the conclusion of the final chapter of this manual.)

FOR FURTHER STUDY

1. Study the ten vanities:

    -Human wisdom: 2:15-16
    -Human labor: 2:19-21
    -Human purpose: 2:26
    -Human rivalry: 4:4
    -Human awareness: 4:7
    -Human fame: 4:16
    -Human dissatisfaction: 5:10
    -Human coveting: 6:9
    -Human frivolity: 7:6
    -Human system of awards: 8:10,14

2. The word "heart" is used 40 times in Ecclesiastes. Read the book to discover what the book has to say about the heart.

3. Make a list of all of Solomon's possessions and experiences in chapter 2. Note in verse 10 that he had "whatever he desired." Observe the results in verse 11: All was vanity. Note the steps which made him realize this: He looked, he turned, he saw, he said in his heart.

4. Study the key word of Ecclesiastes "vanity" which is used 37 times.

5. Note the phrase "under the sun." This is life when spiritual values are ruled out and one dwells only on the world. This phrase occurs 25 times. As you study Ecclesiastes, list Solomon's conclusions about life apart from God (for example, 2:11). Compare this kind of life to the life found in Jesus Christ.

6. The Bible records that King Solomon tried all of the following things trying to give meaning to his life:

-Human wisdom: Ecclesiastes 1:16-18
-Alcohol: Ecclesiastes 2:3
-Pleasure: Ecclesiastes 2:1-3
-Building projects: Ecclesiastes 2:4
-Beautiful gardens and parks: Ecclesiastes 2:4-6
-Personal indulgences: Ecclesiastes 2:7
-Sex: I Kings 11:3

-Wealth: Ecclesiastes 2:7-8
-International reputation: I Kings 10:6-7
-Music: Ecclesiastes 2:8
-Literature: I Kings 4:32
-Military power: I Kings 4:26 and 9:26
-Natural science: I Kings 4:33

CHAPTER TWENTY-THREE

SONG OF SOLOMON

OBJECTIVES:

Upon completion of this chapter you will be able to:

- Name the author of the Song of Solomon.
- Identify to whom the book was written.
- State the purpose for the Song of Solomon.
- Write the Key Verse of the Song of Solomon from memory.
- State the Life and Ministry Principle for the Song of Solomon.

INTRODUCTION

AUTHOR: Solomon

TO WHOM: Israel and all believers

PURPOSE: To show the relationship between Jesus and the Church as demonstrated by the marriage relationship.

KEY VERSE: Song of Solomon 8:7

LIFE AND MINISTRY PRINCIPLE: The divine model of love between a man and his wife is the pattern for relationship between Christ and the Church.

MAIN CHARACTERS: Solomon who represents the bridegroom (Jesus Christ); the Shulamite girl who is the bride (the Church); and the daughters of Jerusalem.

OUTLINE

To understand this book you must realize that it has four levels of interpretation:

1. It is a model of the relationship which should exist between a man and wife.
2. It is an example of God's relationship with His people, Israel.
3. It is an example of the relationship between Christ and the Church.

4. It is an example of the individual relationship between Christ and the believer.

This book is written in dialogue (conversational) form. The best outline for study is in terms of this dialogue. The characters and the order in which they speak are as follows:

CHARACTER	REFERENCE
Bride	1:2-7
Bridegroom	1:8-11
Bride	1:12-14
Bridegroom	1:15
Bride	1:16-17; 2:1
Bridegroom	2:2
Bride	2:3-6
Bridegroom	2:7
Bride	2:8 to the word "me" in verse 10
Bridegroom	2:10 from word "rise" to verse 15
Bride	2:16-17; 3:1-4
Bridegroom	3:5
Bride	3:6-11
Bridegroom	4:1-5
Bride	4:6
Bridegroom	4:7 to the word "out" in verse 16
Bride	4:16 from the word "let"
Bridegroom	5:1
Bride	5:2-8
Daughters of Jerusalem	5:9
Bride	5:10-16
Daughters of Jerusalem	6:1
Bride	6:2-3
Bridegroom	6:4-9
Daughters of Jerusalem	6:10
Bridegroom	6:11-12
Daughters of Jerusalem	6:13
Bridegroom	7:1-9
Bride	7:10-13; 8:1-3
Bridegroom	8:4
Daughters of Jerusalem	8:5 to the word "beloved"
Bridegroom	8:5 from the word "I"
Bride	8:6-8
Bridegroom	8:9
Bride	8:10-12
Bridegroom	8:13
Bride	8:14

SELF-TEST

1. Who was the author of the Song of Solomon?

   _____

2. State the purpose for the Song of Solomon.

   _____

   _____

   _____

3. To whom was the Song of Solomon written?

   _____

   _____

4. State the Life and Ministry Principle of the Song of Solomon.

   _____

   _____

   _____

5. Write the Key Verse of the Song of Solomon.

   _____

   _____

   _____

(Answers to tests are provided at the conclusion of the final chapter in this manual.)

FOR FURTHER STUDY

1. Study the characteristics of the bridegroom as described by the bride. These are natural parallels or descriptions of the spiritual qualities of our bridegroom, the Lord Jesus Christ:

-Swift as a gazelle (animal like a deer) leaping over the hills: 2:9
-Ruddy and handsome, the fairest of ten thousand: 5:10
-His head was covered by wavy, dark hair, pure as gold: 5:11
-His eyes were deep and quiet, like doves beside brooks of water: 5:12
-His lips were like lilies and his breath like myrrh: 5:13
-His cheeks were like sweet beds of spice: 5:13
-His body was bright ivory with jewels: 5:14
-His arms were like round bars of gold set with topaz stones: 5:14
-His legs were like pillars of marble set in sockets of finest gold, like the cedar trees of Lebanon: 5:15

2. Study the natural characteristics of the bride as described by the bridegroom. Remember. . . these are symbolic parallels of spiritual truth. How do these relate to you spiritually as part of the "bride of Christ"?

-She was the most beautiful girl in the world: 1:8
-She was like a bouquet of flowers in a garden: 1:14
-Her eyes were like those of doves: 1:15
-She was like a lily among the thorns: 2:2
-Her hair was like flocks of goats which played across the slopes of Gilead: 4:1
-Her teeth were as white as sheep's wool: 4:2
-Her lips were like a thread of scarlet: 4:3
-Her lips were like honey: 4:11
-Her neck was as stately as the tower of David: 4:4
-Her bosom was like twin fawns feeding among the lilies: 4:5
-She was like a lovely orchard, bearing precious fruit: 4:13
-She was like a garden fountain, a well of living water, refreshing as the streams from the Lebanon mountains: 4:15
-Her thighs were like jewels, the work of the most skilled craftsmen: 7:1
-Her waist was like a heap of wheat set about with lilies: 7:2
-Her navel was as lovely as a goblet filled with wine: 7:2
-Her nose was like the Tower of Lebanon overlooking Damascus: 7:4
-He was overcome by just a glance of her beautiful eyes: 4:9

INTRODUCTION TO THE BOOKS OF PROPHECY

The final group of books in the Old Testament contain the writings of the prophets.

The people of Israel became a nation, were redeemed from slavery in Egypt, and God brought them into their own land. They were given a law to live by, but they were constantly failing in their commitment to God.

With idol worship, civil war, immorality, and unconcern, Israel needed to be recalled again and again to the purpose of their existence. The prophets were men raised up by God to call the people back to God. Several of these books were written during a time period when the nation of Israel was divided into two separate kingdoms: Israel and Judah.

The books of the prophets include the following:

Isaiah: Warns of coming judgment against Judah because of their sins against God.

Jeremiah: Written during the later decline and fall of Judah. Tells of the coming judgment and urges surrender to Nebuchadnezzar.

Lamentations: Jeremiah's lament over Babylon's destruction of Jerusalem.

Ezekiel: Warns first of Jerusalem's impending fall and then foretells its future restoration.

Daniel: The prophet Daniel was captured during the early siege of Judah and taken to Babylon. This book provides both historic and prophetic teaching important in understanding Bible prophecy.

Hosea: Theme of this book is Israel's unfaithfulness, punishment, and restoration.

Joel: Tells of the plagues which foreshadowed future judgment.

Amos: During a period of material prosperity but moral decay, Amos warns Israel and surrounding nations of God's future judgment on their sin.

Obadiah: God's judgment against Edom, an evil nation located south of the Dead Sea.

Jonah: The story of the prophet Jonah who preached repentance in Ninevah, capitol of the Assyrian empire. The book reveals God's love and plan of repentance for the Gentiles.

Micah: Another prophecy against Israel's sin. Foretells the birthplace of Jesus 700 years before the event happened.

Nahum: Tells of the impending destruction of Ninevah which was spared some 150 years earlier through Jonah's preaching.

Habakkuk: Reveals God's plan to punish a sinful nation by an even more sinful one. Teaches that "the just shall live by faith."

Zephaniah: Judgment and restoration of Judah.

Haggai: Urges the Jews to rebuild the temple after a 15 year delay due to enemy resistance.

Zechariah: Further urging to complete the temple and continue spiritual development. Foretells Christ's first and second comings.

Malachi: Warns against spiritual shallowness and foretells the coming of John the Baptist and Jesus.

The chart on the following page tells when and to whom the prophets ministered.

Old Testament Prophets

Prophet	Prophesied To	Dates
Jonah	Assyria	Before Captivity (800-650)
Nahum	Assyria	Before Captivity (800-650)
Obadiah	Edom	Before Captivity (800)
Hosea	Israel	Before Captivity (750)
Amos	Israel	Before Captivity (750)
Isaiah	Judah	Before Captivity (800-606)
Jeremiah/Lamentations	Judah	Before Captivity (800-606)
Joel	Judah	Before Captivity (800-606)
Micah	Judah	Before Captivity (800-606)
Habakkuk	Judah	Before Captivity (800-606)
Zephaniah	Judah	Before Captivity (800-606)
Ezekiel	Judah	During Captivity (606-536)
Daniel	Judah	During Captivity (606-536)
Haggai	Judah	After Captivity (536-400)
Zechariah	Judah	After Captivity (536-400)
Malachi	Judah	After Captivity (536-400)

CHAPTER TWENTY-FOUR

ISAIAH

OBJECTIVES:

Upon completion of this chapter you will be able to:

- Name the author of the book of Isaiah.
- Identify to whom the book of Isaiah was written.
- State the purpose for the book of Isaiah.
- Write the key verse of the book of Isaiah from memory.
- State the Life and Ministry Principle for the book of Isaiah.

INTRODUCTION

AUTHOR: Isaiah

TO WHOM: Judah

PURPOSE: Correction and reproof.

KEY VERSE: Isaiah 53:6

LIFE AND MINISTRY PRINCIPLE: Rebellion leads to retribution. Repentance leads to restoration.

MAIN CHARACTERS: Isaiah, Hezekiah

OUTLINE

Part One

I. Prophecies concerning Judah and Jerusalem: 1:1-12:6

    A. General introduction: 1:1-31
    B. Millennial blessing by cleansing: 2:1-4:6
    C. Punishment for Israel's sins: 5:1-30
    D. The prophet's call and commission: 6:1-13
    E. The prophecy of Immanuel: 7:1-25
    F. The prophecy of the Assyrian invasion: 8:1-22

- G. Messianic prediction and warning: 9:1-21
- H. Punishment of Assyria: 10:1-34
- I. Restoration and blessing: 11:1-16
- J. Worship: 12:1-6

II. Prophecies against foreign nations: 13:1-23:18
- A. Babylon: 13:1-14:23
- B. Assyria: 14:24-27
- C. Philistia: 14:28-32
- D. Moab: 15:1-16:14
- E. Damascus: 17:1-14
- F. Land beyond the rivers of Ethiopia: 18:1-7
- G. Egypt: 19:1-25
- H. Egypt and Ethiopia: 20:1-6
- I. Dumah: 21:11-12
- J. Arabia: 21:13-17
- K. Valley of vision: 22:1-25
- L. Tyre: 23:1-18

III. Prophecy of the establishment of the Kingdom: 24:1-27:13
- A. The tribulation: 24:1-23
- B. The character of the kingdom: 25:1-12
- C. The testimony of restored Israel: 26:1-27:13

IV. Prophecy concerning Judah in relation to Assyria:
- A. The fall of Samaria: 28:1-13
- B. Warning to Judah: 28:14-29
- C. The attack of Zion: 29:1-4
- D. The attacker frustrated: 29:5-8
- E. Reasons for the trial: 29:9-16
- F. Blessings of final deliverance: 29:17-24
- G. Warning against an Egyptian alliance: 30:1-14
- H. Exhortation to rely on God for help: 30:15-31:9
- I. The day of the Lord: 34:1-17
- J. The kingdom blessing: 35:1-10

Connecting Link

Chapters 36 through 39 are a historical transition from the Assyrian to the Babylonian period:

I. Sennacherib's invasion: 36:1-37:38
II. Hezekiah's sickness and recovery: 38:1-22
III. Arrival of Babylonian envoy and captivity: 39:1-8

Part Two

I. Comfort of the Exiles in the promise of restoration: 40:1-66:24

   A. The promise of restoration: 40:1-11
   B. The basis of comfort: God's character: 40:12-31
   C. The reason for comfort: 41:1-29
   D. The Comforter: 42:1-25
   E. The results of the comfort: 43:1-47:15
      1. The nation restored: 43:1-45:25
      2. The downfall of idols of Babylon: 46:1-13
      3. Downfall of Babylon: 47:1-15
   F. Exhortation of comfort for those who are delivered from captivity: 48:1-22

II. Comfort of the exiles with the prophecy of Jesus the Redeemer: 49:1-57:21

   A. Call and work: 49:1-26
   B. Obedience and faithfulness: 50:1-11
   C. Redemption of Israel: 51:1-52:12
   D. Atonement and exaltation: 52:13-53:12
   E. Israel's restoration: 54:1-17
   F. Worldwide salvation: 55:1-13
   G. His warnings and promises: 56:1-57:21

III. Comfort of the exiles with the prophecy of the future glory of Israel: 58:1-66:24

   A. Obstacles to the restoration and their removal: 58:1-59:21
   B. Glory of Jerusalem in the Messianic age: 60:1-22
   C. Blessings of the Messiah for Israel and the world: 61:1-11
   D. God's love for Jerusalem and its results: 62:1-12
   E. Christ's conquest of Israel's enemies results in acknowledgment of past national deliverances: 63:1-14
   F. Prayer of the remnant: 63:15-64:12
   G. God's answer: 65:1-25
   H. Blessings of the Messianic Kingdom: 66:1-24

SELF-TEST

1. Who was the author of the book of Isaiah?

   _____

2. State the purpose for the book of Isaiah.

   _____

   _____

   _____

3. To whom was the book of Isaiah written?

   _____

   _____

4. State the Life and Ministry Principle of the book of Isaiah.

   _____

   _____

   _____

   _____

5. Write the Key Verse of Isaiah.

   _____

   _____

   _____

   _____

(Answers to tests are provided at the conclusion of the final chapter in this manual.)

FOR FURTHER STUDY

1. The book of Isaiah can be compared to the Bible:

-The Bible has 66 books. Isaiah has 66 chapters.

-The Old Testament has 39 books covering the history and sin Israel. The first section of Isaiah has 39 chapters on the same subject.

-The New Testament has 27 books describing the ministry of Jesus Christ. The last section of Isaiah has 27 chapters focusing on this subject.

-The New Testament begins with the ministry of John the Baptist. The second section of Isaiah begins by predicting his ministry.

-The New Testament ends by describing the new heavens and earth. Isaiah ends by describing the same things.

2. Isaiah includes several important passages:

    -The only Old Testament prophecy concerning the virgin birth of Jesus: Isaiah 7:14
    -One of the clearest statements on the Trinity: 48:16
    -The most important chapter of the entire Old Testament: 53

3. Study the use of the word "salvation" in Isaiah. It appears 33 times in this book.

4. Important subjects to study in Isaiah:

    -What the book reveals about the character of God.
    -What the book reveals of the ministry of Jesus.
    -The tribulation.
    -The Millennium reign of Jesus Christ.

5. Spiritual keys to Isaiah's ministry:

    -Conviction: 6:5   -Consecration: 6:8
    -Confession: 6:5   -Commission: 6:9
    -Cleansing: 6:7

CHAPTER TWENTY-FIVE

JEREMIAH

OBJECTIVES:

Upon completion of this chapter you will be able to:

- Name the author of the book of Jeremiah.
- Identify to whom the book of Jeremiah was written.
- State the purpose for the book of Jeremiah.
- Write memory, the Key Verses of the book of Jeremiah from memory.
- State the Life and Ministry Principle for the book of Jeremiah.

INTRODUCTION

AUTHOR: Jeremiah

TO WHOM: Judah

PURPOSE: To warn of the coming judgment of captivity and call for repentance.

KEY VERSES: Jeremiah 33:3 and 1:7-8

LIFE AND MINISTRY PRINCIPLE: National disasters and deteriorations are often due to disobedience to God.

MAIN CHARACTER: Jeremiah

OUTLINE

I. Introduction: The Prophet's call: 1:1-19

II. Prophecies against Judah and Jerusalem: 2:1-45:5

    A. Prophecies during the reigns of Josiah and Jehoiakim: 1:1-20:18
        1. First prophecy: Sin and ingratitude of the nation: 2:1-3:5
        2. Second prophecy: Destruction from the north: 3:6-6:30

3. Third prophecy: Threat of exile: 7:1-10:25
4. Fourth prophecy: The broken covenant and the sign of the girdle: 11:1-13:27
5. Fifth prophecy: 14:1-17:27
   a. The drought: 14:1-15:21
   b. The unmarried prophet: 16:1-17:18
   c. The warning concerning the Sabbath: 17:19-27
6. The sixth prophecy: The sign the potter's house: 18:1-20:18

B. Prophecies at various periods before the fall of Jerusalem: 21:1-39:18
   1. Punishment upon Zedekiah and the people: 21:1-29:32
   2. Future Messianic Kingdom: 30:1-33:26
   3. Zedekiah's sin and loyalty of the Rechabites: 34:1-35:19
   4. Jehoiakim's opposition: 36:1-32
   5. Jeremiah's experiences during the siege: 37:1-39:18

C. Prophecies after the fall of Jerusalem: 40:1-45:5
   1. Jeremiah's ministry among the remnant: 40:1-42:22
   2. Jeremiah's ministry in Egypt: 43:1-44:30
   3. Jeremiah's message to Baruch: 45:1-5

III. Prophecies against the nations: 46:1-51:64

   A. Against Egypt: 46:1-28
   B. Against Philistia: 47:1-7
   C. Against Moab: 48:1-47
   D. Against Ammon: 49:1-6
   E. Against Edom: 49:7-22
   F. Against Damascus: 49:23-27
   G. Against Arabia: 49:28-33
   H. Against Elam: 49:34-39
   I. Against Babylon: 50:1-51:64

IV. Appendix: Fall and liberation: 52:1-52:34

   A. The fall and captivity of Judah: 52:1-30
   B. The liberation: 52:31-34

SELF-TEST

1. Who was the author of the book of Jeremiah?

   _____

2. State the purpose for the book of Jeremiah.

   _____

   _____

   _____

3. To whom was the book of Jeremiah written?

   _____

   _____

4. State the Life and Ministry Principle of the book of Jeremiah.

   _____

   _____

   _____

5. Write the Key Verses of Jeremiah.

   _____

   _____

   _____

(Answers to tests are provided at the conclusion of the final chapter in this manual.)

FOR FURTHER STUDY

1. Several object lessons are used by Jeremiah. An object lesson is when a visible object is used to illustrate a spiritual truth. Study these object lessons in the book of Jeremiah in the chapters indicated:

    -An almond rod: 1
    -Boiling caldron: 1
    -Marred girdle: 13
    -Full bottle: 13
    -Drought: 14
    -Potter's vessel: 18
    -Broken bottle: 19
    -Two baskets of figs: 24
    -Bonds and bars: 27
    -Buying a field: 32
    -Hidden stones: 43
    -A book sunk in the river: 51

2. Jeremiah was the only Biblical prophet who was forbidden to pray for his nation: 7:16; 11:14; 14:11; 16:5

3. The sufferings of Jeremiah were similar to the sufferings of Jesus:

-Both were mistreated by their families: Jeremiah 12:6, John 7:5

-Both were plotted against by citizens of their own home towns: Jeremiah 11:21, Luke 4:28-30

-Both were hated by the religious world: Jeremiah 26:7-8, John 11:47-53

-Both were denounced by synagogue leaders: Jeremiah 20:1, John 18:13,24

-Both were aided by a king: Jeremiah 38:16, Luke 23:4

-Both were described similarly: Jeremiah 11:19, Isaiah 53:7

-Both wept over Jerusalem: Jeremiah 9:1, Luke 19:41

-Both predicted the destruction of the Temple: Jeremiah 7:11-15, Matthew 24:1-2

CHAPTER TWENTY-SIX

LAMENTATIONS

OBJECTIVES:

Upon completion of this chapter you will be able to:

- Name the author of the book of Lamentations.
- Identify to whom the book of Lamentations was written.
- State the purpose for the book of Lamentations.
- Write the Key Verses of the book of Lamentations from memory.
- State the Life and Ministry Principle for the book of Lamentations.

INTRODUCTION

AUTHOR: Jeremiah

TO WHOM: Jews who were captive in Babylon

PURPOSE: To produce repentance necessary for spiritual restoration.

KEY VERSES: Lamentations 3:22-23

LIFE AND MINISTRY PRINCIPLE: God is faithful in both judgment and mercy.

MAIN CHARACTER: Jeremiah

OUTLINE

I. The condition of Jerusalem: 1:1-22
　Note the following verses of indictment: 1:1,3,8,9,17

II. Punishment from God: The results described: 2:1-22

　　A. God had destroyed every home in Judah: 2:1-2
　　B. Every fortress and wall was broken: 2:2
　　C. His bow of judgment was bent across the land: 2:4
　　D. The Temple had fallen: 2:6

  E. Judah's enemies were given freedom to destroy: 2:15-16
  F. Bodies of the people lined the streets of Jerusalem: 2:21-22

III. The prophet of God: 3:1-66

  A. The affliction of the prophet: 3:1-19
  B. The assurance of the prophet: 3:21-27, 31-33
  C. The advice of the prophet: 3:40-66

IV. Description of conditions continued: 4:1-22
  A. Children are thirsty: 4:4
  B. Youth treated badly: 5:13
  C. Rich were in the streets begging: 4:5
  D. Formerly mighty princes were now thin with blackened faces: 4:7,8
  E. Women had cooked and eaten their own children: 4:10
  F. False prophets and priests were blindly staggering through the streets: 4:14
  G. King Zedekiah had been captured, blinded, and carried into captivity: 4:20

V. The prayer of the prophet: 5:1-18

It was a prayer of:
  A. Remembrance: 5:1
  B. Repentance: 5:16
  C. Recognition of God: 5:19
  D. Renewal: 5:21

SELF-TEST

1. Who was the author of the book of Lamentations?
   _____

2. State the purpose for the book of Lamentations.
   _____
   _____
   _____

3. To whom was the book of Lamentations written?
   _____
   _____

4. State the Life and Ministry Principle of the book of Lamentations.
   _____
   _____
   _____

5. Write the Key Verses of Lamentations.
   _____
   _____
   _____

(Answers to tests are provided at the conclusion of the final chapter in this manual.)

FOR FURTHER STUDY

1. One of the greatest passages on the faithfulness of God is found in Lamentations 3:21-33. Compare this with II Timothy 2:13.

2. Compare Revelation 18 to the book of Lamentations. In Lamentations, the prophet weeps over the destruction of the Messianic city of Jerusalem. In Revelation 18, the merchants weep over the destruction of the materialistic city of Babylon.

3. Read Lamentations 5:16. This verse summarizes the reasons for God's judgment. Around 1000 B.C. David established his capital in Jerusalem. God blessed this city for nearly 400 years and spared it even after he allowed the northern kingdom to be carried away by the Assyrians in 721 B.C. All of His mercy was in vain, however, for the people of Judah continued to sin. Judgment now came.

4. The Jews have for centuries publicly read Lamentations each year on the ninth month of Ab to commemorate the destruction of the first Temple in 586 B.C. and the second Temple in A.D. 70.

5. It is said that Jeremiah sat weeping outside the north wall of Jerusalem under a hill called Golgotha where Christ would later die.

6. Jerusalem is personified as a woman. List what happened to Jerusalem and why. Note her emotions, the anguish because of her children, and the thoughts and memories she must deal with.

7. Record what you learn about God in this book: His character, His judgments, and why He acts as He does. For example Lamentations 1:5 states that God caused Judah grief because of her sin and brought about her captivity because of her transgressions.

8. Why do you think God deals with sin as He does? How should we respond? Read chapter 3 so your "dancing" will not be turned into "mourning."

CHAPTER TWENTY-SEVEN

EZEKIEL

OBJECTIVES:

Upon completion of this chapter you will be able to:
- Name the author of the book of Ezekiel.
- Identify to whom the book of Ezekiel was written.
- State the purpose for the book of Ezekiel.
- Write the Key Verse of the book of Ezekiel from memory.
- State the Life and Ministry Principle for the book of Ezekiel.

INTRODUCTION

AUTHOR: Ezekiel

TO WHOM: Judah

PURPOSE: Ezekiel warned of the coming captivity, then prophesied to the captives after it occurred.

KEY VERSE: Ezekiel 22:30

LIFE AND MINISTRY PRINCIPLE: The Lord orders historical events so that the nations will know He is God.

MAIN CHARACTER: Ezekiel

OUTLINE

Part One: Prophecies Before The Siege Of Jerusalem--Chapters 1-24

Six years before the destruction of Jerusalem, Ezekiel began his prophecies of warning to Judah.

I. The prophet's call and commission: 1:1-3:27

    A. The vision: 1:1-28
    B. The call: 2:1-3:27

II. Prophecies against Judah and Jerusalem: 4:1-24:27

    A. Destruction predicted: 4:1-7:27
        1. By sign and symbol: 4:1-5:17
        2. By prophecies: 6:1-7:27
    B. Jerusalem's sin and punishment: 8:1-11:25
        1. Vision of sin: 8:1-18
        2. Punishment: 9:1-11:25
    C. Necessity of punishment: 12:1-19:14
    D. Last warning before the fall: 20:1-24:27

Part Two: Prophecies During The Siege Of Jerusalem--Chapters 25-32

These prophecies were directed at Judah's enemies.

I. Prophecies against surrounding nations: 25:1-32:32

    A. Against Ammon: 25:1-7
    B. Against Moab: 25:8-11
    C. Against Edom: 25:12-14
    D. Against Philistia: 25:15-17
    E. Against Tyre: 26:1-28:19
    F. Against Sidon: 28:20-26
    G. Against Egypt: 29:1-32:32

Part Three: Prophecies After The Siege Of Jerusalem--Chapters 33-48

These prophecies concerned the restoration of Judah.

I. Events preceding the establishment of the Kingdom: 33:1-39:29

    A. The wicked purged: 33:1-33
    B. False shepherds give way to the true shepherd: 34:1-31
    C. Restoration of the land: 36:1-15
    D. Restoration of the people: 36:16-37:28
    E. Judgment of Israel's enemies: 38:1-39:24
    F. The restored nation: 39:25-29

II. The Millennial Kingdom: 40:1-48:35

    A. The temple: 40:1-43:27
    B. The worship: 44:1-46:24
    C. The land: 47:1-48:35

SELF-TEST

1. Who was the author of the book of Ezekiel?

   _____

2. State the purpose for the book of Ezekiel.

   _____

   _____

   _____

3. To whom was the book of Ezekiel written?

   _____

   _____

4. State the Life and Ministry Principle of the book of Ezekiel.

   _____

   _____

   _____

5. Write the Key Verse of Ezekiel from memory.

   _____

   _____

   _____

(Answers to tests are provided at the conclusion of the final chapter in this manual.)

FOR FURTHER STUDY

1. Compare Ezekiel chapter 16 and the book of Hosea.

2. The most vivid Old Testament vision is the valley of dry bones found in Ezekiel 37. Study this chapter.

3. This book describes one of seven Biblical temples, the Millennial temple. See Ezekiel chapters 40-48. Read about the other Biblical temples in these chapters:

-The tabernacle of Moses: Exodus 40
-The temple of Solomon: I Kings 6
-The temple of Zerubbabel/Herod: Ezra 6, John 2
-The temple of Christ's body: John 2
-The spiritual temple: The church: Acts 2
-The tribulation temple: Revelation 11

4. It is important to realize that God orders the events of history with one purpose in mind: That the nations might know He is the true God. The phrase "they shall known I am Jehovah" occurs 70 times in this book. Underline these passages as you study Ezekiel to help you understand the divine purpose of God's actions.

5. Ezekiel is a prophet of visions. He wrote that as he was among the captives, "...the heavens were opened, and I saw visions of God" (Ezekiel 1:1). Here are the visions he saw:

   -The vision of the Cherubim: Ezekiel 1:1-3:13
   -The vision of glory and godlessness: Ezekiel 8:1-11:25
   -The vision of the burning vine: Ezekiel 15:18
   -The vision of dry bones: Ezekiel 37:1-28

6. Parables and signs in Ezekiel:

-The parable of the two eagles reveals the King of Babylon and the King of Egypt; the highest branch corresponds to Jehoiachin; seed of the land was Zedekiah; the tender twig stood for the Messiah: Ezekiel chapter 17

-Chapters 20-23 include several parables. One of the most important is that of the two sisters, Aholah and Aholibah. They represent Israel and Judah's deterioration into idolatry.

-The parable of the boiling caldron symbolizes the condition of Jerusalem when the Babylonians invade it: Ezekiel 11:1-13

-Two sticks, one Judah and the other Israel, are shown as ultimately reunited under the Shepherd King: Ezekiel 37:1-28

CHAPTER TWENTY-EIGHT

DANIEL

OBJECTIVES:

Upon completion of this chapter you will be able to:

- Name the author of the book of Daniel.
- Identify to whom the book of Daniel was written.
- State the purpose for the book of Daniel.
- Write the Key Verse of the book of Daniel from memory.
- State the Life and Ministry Principle for the book of Daniel.

INTRODUCTION

AUTHOR: Daniel

TO WHOM: The Jewish captives

PURPOSE: To show how God rules the affairs of men.

KEY VERSE: Daniel 12:3

LIFE AND MINISTRY PRINCIPLE: God is sovereign and He honors those who honor Him.

MAIN CHARACTER: Daniel

OUTLINE

I. Introductory background: The reasons for Daniel's prosperity: 1:1-21

II. Visions and events under Nebuchadnezzar: 2:1-6:28

    A. The image and interpretation: 2:1-49
       Four kingdoms or world empires:
       1. Babylonian: 606 B.C.
       2. Medo-Persian: 538 B.C.

            3. Grecian: 330 B.C.
            4. Roman: 63 B.C.
    B. The fiery furnace: 3:1-30
        1. The king's command: 3:1-7
        2. The stand of God's men: 3:8-23
        3. Judgment and deliverance: 3:24-30
    C. Nebuchadnezzar's tree vision and its meaning: 4:1-37
        1. The dream: 4:1-18
        2. The interpretation: 4:19-27
        3. The fulfillment: 4:28-37
    D. Belshazzar's feast: 5:1-31
        1. The feast: 5:1-4
        2. The judgment: 5:5-9
        3. The search for an interpreter: 5:10-16
        4. The interpretation: 5:17-29
        5. The fulfillment: 5:30-31
    E. Daniel's deliverance from the lions' den: 6:1-28
        1. An evil plan: 6:1-9
        2. Daniel's response: 6:10-20
        3. Deliverance from the den: 6:21-28

III. Visions under Belshazzar, Darius, and Cyrus: 7:1-12:13

    A. The four beasts and interpretation: 7:1-28
        1. They arise from a great sea: 7:1-3
            (a) Beast like a lion: Babylon: 7:4
            (b) Beast like a bear: Medo-Persia: 7:5
            (c) Beast like a leopard: Greece: 7:6
            (d) Beast like a monster: Rome: 7:7
        2. The little horn (antichrist): 7:8
        3. Kingdom of God: 7:9-14
        4. Interpretation: 7:15-28
    B. The ram and the goat and interpretation: 8:1-27
        1. The introduction: 8:1-2
        2. The vision: 8:3-14
            (a) The ram is Medo-Persia: 8:3-4
            (b) The goat is Greece: 8:5-14
        3. Revelations concerning Antiochus Epiphanes and the Anti-Christ: 8:15-27
    C. The seventy weeks: 9:1-27
        1. Introduction: 9:1-2
        2. The prayer: 9:3-19
        3. The seventy weeks: 9:20-27

D. Preparation for the final revelation: 10:1-21
   1. Introduction: 10:1-3
   2. The man clothed in linen: 10:4-6
   3. Daniel's response: 10:10-12
   4. Conflict of Gabriel and the Prince of Persia: 10:13
   5. Reason for the angel's coming: 10:14-21
E. Vision of events from Darius to the end of time: 11:1-12:13
   1. The revelation of events to come: 11:1-12:3
   2. The command to seal the book: 12:4
   3. A final conversation with the messenger: 12:5-13

SELF-TEST

1. Who was the author of the book of Daniel?

   _____

2. State the purpose for the book of Daniel.

   _____

   _____

   _____

3. To whom was the book of Daniel written?

   _____

   _____

4. State the Life and Ministry Principle of the book of Daniel.

   _____

   _____

   _____

5. Write the Key Verse of Daniel.

   _____

   _____

   _____

(Answers to tests are provided at the conclusion of the final chapter in this manual.)

FOR FURTHER STUDY

1. Ezekiel refers to Daniel. He compares him to Noah and Job: Ezekiel 14:14. He also refers to the wisdom of Daniel: Ezekiel 28:3. Jesus quoted Daniel: Matthew 24:15

2. Daniel contains a great prayer of personal confession: 9:3-19

3. Important things in Daniel:

    -The most dramatic feast in the Bible: 5

    -The only Old Testament description of the Father: 7:9-14

    -The only book mentioning both Gabriel and Michael (Heaven's two archangels): 9:21; 10:13; 12:1

    -An explanation as to why prayer might sometimes be hindered: 10:10-13

    -The most complete description of the Antichrist: 7:7-27; 8:23-25; 9:26; 11:36-45

4. The 70 weeks of Daniel described in 9:24-27 uses the word "week" to mean a period of 70 years. If there are 70 seven year periods, it equals 490 years. The division of these years are as follows:

    -7 weeks, or 49 years, began at the command to build Jerusalem under Ezra and Nehemiah.

    -62 weeks, or 434 years, began at the building of the wall of Jerusalem and continued to the time of the crucifixion when Jesus was "cut off."

    -Gentile rule, an unknown number of years intervenes after the 69th week. We are in this period now, awaiting the return of Jesus.

    -70th week, 7 years not yet begun, during which God deals with Israel. This starts when the Antichrist takes power and the tribulation begins. This ushers in the time of trouble of Daniel 12:1 which is the great tribulation described in Revelation.

5. The rise and fall of world empires discussed in Daniel chapters 2, 7, and 8 is summarized on the following page:

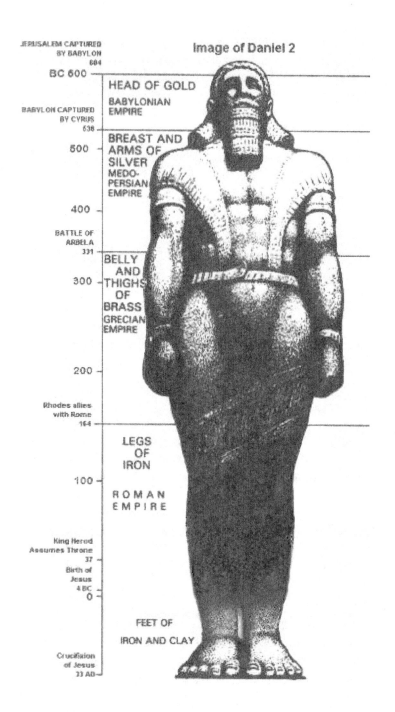

CHAPTER TWENTY-NINE

HOSEA

OBJECTIVES:

Upon completion of this chapter you will be able to:

- Name the author of the book of Hosea.
- Identify to whom the book of Hosea was written.
- State the purpose for the book of Hosea.
- Write the Key Verse of the book of Hosea from memory.
- State the Life and Ministry Principle for the book of Hosea.

INTRODUCTION

AUTHOR: Hosea

TO WHOM: Northern kingdom of Israel.

PURPOSE: To alert Israel to her sinful condition and bring her back to God.

KEY VERSE: Hosea 4:1

LIFE AND MINISTRY PRINCIPLE: Experience fosters understanding and compassion.

MAIN CHARACTERS: Hosea, Gomer, Jezreel, Lo-Ruhamah, Lo-Ammi

OUTLINE

I. Introduction: 1:1

II. The symbolic example: 1:1-2:23

    A. Israel rejected: Hosea's marriage and birth of children.
        1. Charged to take a wife of whoredom: 1:2-3
        2. Jezreel symbolizes the overthrow of Jehu's dynasty: 1:4-5
        3. Lo-ruhamah: God will no more have mercy on Israel: 1:6-7
        4. Lo-ammi: Utter rejection of Israel: 1:8-9
    B. Israel comforted: 1:10-11
    C. Israel chastised: 2:1-13

            1.   Condemnation of sinful conduct: 2:1-7
            2.   Punishment more fully explained: 2:8-13
     D.   Israel restored: 2:14-23
            1.   Promise of conversion: 2:14-17
            2.   Renewal of covenant: 2:18-23

III.   Redemption of an adulterous wife: 3:1-5

     A.   Hosea's experience: 3:1-3
     B.   Israel's parallel experience: 3:4-5

IV.   The triumph of divine love in the restoration of a repentant nation: 4:1-14:9
     A.   Israel's guilt: 4:1-19
            1.   The general charge: 4:1-5
            2.   Willful ignorance: 4:6-11
            3.   Idolatry: 4:12-19
     B.   The divine displeasure: 5:1-15
            1.   Guilt of priests, people, princes: 5:1-7
            2.   Judgment will follow: 5:8-15
     C.   The repentant remnant: 6:1-3
            1.   Return, but without heartfelt repentance: 6:1-3
     D.   The response of God: 6:4-13:8
            1.   God is not deceived: 6:4-11
     E.   National government corrupt: 7:1-7
     F.   Foreign policy corrupt: 7:8-16
     G.   Consequences of national corruption: 8:1-14
     H.   The apostasy and its punishment: 9:1-9
     I.   As God found Israel and as they became: 9:10-17
     J.   Puppet kings and gods: 10:1-3
     K.   Righteousness becomes poison: 10:4-5
     L.   Assyria used in judgment: 10:6-7
     M.   The terror of judgment: 10:8
     N.   Persistence in rebellion: 10:9-15
     O.   Ingratitude for God's love: 11:1-7
     P.   Israel's Canaanitish ways: 11:12-12:14
     Q.   Idolatry the basis of destruction: 13:1-8

V. The final restoration: 13:9-14:9

    A. Distrust in God: 13:9-1.
    B. Call to repentance: 14:1-3
    C. Promise of healing and Epilogue--Israel repents, God hears: 14:4-9

SELF-TEST

1. Who was the author of the book of Hosea?

   _____

2. State the purpose for the book of Hosea.

   _____

   _____

   _____

3. To whom was the book of Hosea written?

   _____

   _____

4. State the Life and Ministry Principle of the book of Hosea.

   _____

   _____

   _____

5. Write the Key Verse of Hosea.

   _____

   _____

   _____

(Answers to tests are provided at the conclusion of the final chapter in this manual.)

FOR FURTHER STUDY

1. Read II Kings 14:23-17:41. This passage describes the time during which Hosea prophesied.

2. The following examples of sin are used by God in the book of Hosea:

   -An adulterous wife: 3:1
   -A drunkard: 4:11
   -A backsliding heifer: 4:16
   -Troops of robbers: 6:9
   -Adulterers: 7:4
   -A smoldering oven: 7:7
   -A cake half-baked: 7:8
   -A silly dove: 7:11
   -A deceitful bow: 7:16
   -Swallowed up: 8:8
   -A vessel: 8:8
   -A wild ass: 8:9

3. Why would God tell a man to marry a prostitute? There were several reasons:

   First, by marrying an unfaithful wife Hosea understood through experience the anguish in God's heart. God's people were committing spiritual adultery. Second, Hosea's own marriage was a living visual illustration of God's message to Israel. Third, God commanded Hosea to name his children by titles which described the future punishment and eventual restoration of Israel.

4. Israel's list of sins recorded in Hosea: -Falsehood: 4:1 -Robbery: 7:1 -Murder: 5:2 -Oppression: 12:7 -Licentiousness (unrestrained by law or morality): :11

5. Hosea used hard language to drive home the message God gave him. He used the word whoredom(s) fourteen times; lovers six times; harlot(s) four times; various forms of the word adultery six times; a whoring two times; lewdness two times; and the word whores once.

6. Hosea used three figures to emphasize the relation of God to His people: The example of a father and son (11:1); a husband and wife (2:16); and a king and his subjects (13:10).

CHAPTER THIRTY

JOEL

OBJECTIVES:

Upon completion of this chapter you will be able to:

- Name the author of the book of Joel.
- Identify to whom the book of Joel was written.
- State the purpose for the book of Joel.
- Write the Key Verses of the book of Joel from memory.
- State the Life and Ministry Principle for the book of Joel.

INTRODUCTION

AUTHOR: Joel

TO WHOM: Judah

PURPOSE: To warn Judah of their sin and need for repentance and inform of God's future plans for the nation. A first judgment (1:2-2:17) precedes a greater judgment to follow (2:18-3:21).

KEY VERSES: Joel 2:28-29

LIFE AND MINISTRY PRINCIPLE: Even in the midst of corrective judgment, God plans future blessings for His people.

MAIN CHARACTER: Joel

OUTLINE

I.   The prophet presented: 1:1

II. A type of the "day of the Lord": 1:2-20

    A.   The locust plague: 1:2-7
    B.   The people exhorted to repent: 1:8-20
           1.   The elders (leaders): 1:2

            2. Old and young: 1:2-3
            3. Drunkards: 1:5-7
            4. Whole nation: 1:8-12
            5. Priests (ministers): 1:9
            6. Husbandmen: Laborers: 1:10-12
    C. Exhortation to repent: 1:13-14
    D. "Day of Jehovah": Prayer for mercy: 1:15-20 Note that we are to . . .
            1. Hear: 1:1
            2. Awake: 1:5
            3. Lament: 1:8
            4. Be ashamed: 1:11
            5. Gird in sackcloth: 1:13
            6. Sanctify a fast: 1:14
            7. Call a solemn assembly of repentance: 1:15
            8. Cry unto the Lord: 1:14,19

III. The "day of the Lord": 2:1-32

    A. The invading northern army: 2:1-10
    B. God's army at Armageddon: 2:11
    C. The repentant remnant: 2:12-17
            1. Rend the heart, not the garments: 2:12-14
            2. Sincerely repent and fervently pray: 2:15-17
    D. God's response to the remnant: 2:18-29
            1. Repentance: 2:18
            2. Restoration: 2:19-27
            3. Outpouring of Spirit: 2:28-29
            4. Judgment on the wicked: 2:20,30-31
            5. Escape of the remnant in Zion: 2:32
    E. Signs preceding the "day of the Lord": 2:30-32

IV. The judgment of the nations: 3:1-16

    A. Israel restored: 3:1
    B. The nations judged: 3:2-3
    C. The Phoenicians and Philistines especially condemned: 3:4-8
    D. The nations challenged to war and judgment: 3:9-16

V. The prophecy of the kingdom blessing: 3:17-21
    A. The exaltation of Jerusalem: 3:17
    B. Judah's prosperity: 3:18
    C. Egypt and Edom's desolation: 3:19
    D. Jerusalem's exaltation explained: 3:20-21

SELF-TEST

1. Who was the author of the book of Joel?

2. State the purpose for the book of Joel.

3. To whom was the book of Joel written?

4. State the Life and Ministry Principle of the book of Joel.

5. From memory, write the Key Verses of Joel.

(Answers to tests are provided at the conclusion of the final chapter in this manual.)

FOR FURTHER STUDY

1. Joel was the first prophet to use the phrase "the day of the Lord." This title describes the seven-year tribulation period which will come upon the earth at the time of God's final judgment. Read about "the day of the Lord" in Joel 1:15; 2:1,11,31; and 3:14.

2. Here is a summary of the condition of Judah as described by Joel:

    -Destroyed by enemy: 1:4,6-7
    -New wine cut off: 1:6,10
    (Jesus is the vine; the people were cut off from the vine, the source of life.)
    -Harvest perishing: 1:11-12
    -Left first love: 1:8
    -Offerings cut off: 1:9
    -Ministers mourning: 1:9
    -Joy gone: 1:12,16
    -Spiritually hungry: 1:17-20

3. Here is the remedy God gives by Joel:

    -Repentance: 2:12-13
    -Recognition of God: 2:26
    -Relation (come to know God): 2:27
    -Reverence for God: 2:27 ("I am the Lord; none beside me")

4. If Judah repented, here is what would happen:

    -Restoration: 2:25
    -Revival and refreshing: 2:23
    -Revelation: 2:28-31
    -Redemption (salvation) and release (deliverance): 2:32
    -Readiness (prepared, not ashamed): 3:13-14

CHAPTER THIRTY-ONE

AMOS

OBJECTIVES:

Upon completion of this chapter you will be able to:

- Name the author of the book of Amos.
- Identify to whom the book of Amos was written.
- State the purpose for the book of Amos.
- Write the Key Verse of the book of Amos from memory.
- State the Life and Ministry Principle for the book of Amos.

INTRODUCTION

AUTHOR: Amos

TO WHOM: Israel

PURPOSE: To call Israel back to God.

KEY VERSE: Amos 4:12

LIFE AND MINISTRY PRINCIPLE: The call to the nations is still "Prepare to meet thy God."

MAIN CHARACTER: Amos

OUTLINE

I. Introduction: 1:1-2

II. Judgment upon nations neighboring Israel: 1:3-2:3

    A. Damascus 1:3-5
    B. Philistia: 1:6-8
    C. Phoenicia: 1:9-10

- D. Edom: 1:11-12
- E. Ammon: 1:13-15
- F. Moab: 2:1-3

III. Judgment on Judah and Israel: 2:4-16

- A. On Judah: 2:4-5
- B. On Israel: 2:6-16

IV. God's indictment of the family of Jacob: 3:1-9:10

- A. Three addresses of condemnation: 3:1-6:15
  1. Judgment is deserved: 3:1-10
     Judgment is decreed: 3:11-15
  2. Judgment is deserved: 4:1-11
     Judgment is decreed: 4:12-13
  3. Judgment is deserved: 5:1-15
     Judgment is decreed: 5:16-6:14
- B. Five symbolic visions of punishments: 7:1-9:10
  1. The locust: 7:1-3
  2. The drought: 7:4-6
  3. The plumb line with a historical reference: 7:7-17
  4. The fruit basket: 8:1-14
  5. The Lord standing on the altar: 9:1-10

V. Hope for a brighter future: 9:11-15

- A. Christ's return and establishment of the Messianic reign: 9:11-12
- B. Millennial prosperity: 9:13
- C. Israel restored: 9:14-15

SELF-TEST

1. Who was the author of the book of Amos?

   _____

2. State the purpose for the book of Amos.

   _____
   _____
   _____

3. To whom was the book of Amos written?

   _____
   _____

4. State the Life and Ministry Principle of the book of Amos.

   _____
   _____
   _____

5. Write the Key Verse of Amos.

   _____
   _____
   _____

(Answers to tests are provided at the conclusion of the final chapter in this manual.)

FOR FURTHER STUDY

1. The watchful eye of God sees:

    -Past sin: 1:3
    -Individual acts: 1:6
    -Broken promises: 1:9
    -Hidden enmity of the heart: 1:11
    -Emotions and ambition: 1:13
    -Memory and its treasured sins: 2:1

2. Amos deals with five features of the day of the Lord:

    -The King: 9:11
    -The nations: 9:12
    -The earth: 9:13
    -The people: 9:14
    -The land: 9:15

3. The first part of Amos is bracketed between two references to the roaring lion in 1:2 and 3:8. The lion first denounces the sins of the Gentile world (1:3-2:3), then the Israelite world (southern kingdom of Judah 2:4-5 and northern kingdom of Israel 2:6, 16), and ends by binding them together in a final oracle (3:1-2).

4. List all the nations mentioned in the book of Amos, the reason for their punishment, and the judgment which was to come:

Nation	Reasons For Punishment	Judgment To Come

CHAPTER THIRTY-TWO

OBADIAH

OBJECTIVES:

Upon completion of this chapter you will be able to:

- Name the author of the book of Obadiah.
- Identify to whom the book of Obadiah was written.
- State the purpose for the book of Obadiah.
- Write the Key Verse of the book of Obadiah from memory.
- State the Life and Ministry Principle for the book of Obadiah.

INTRODUCTION

AUTHOR: Obadiah

TO WHOM: The nation of Edom.

PURPOSE: To warn of God's punishment for sin.

KEY VERSE: Obadiah 1:4

LIFE AND MINISTRY PRINCIPLE: God brings down that which has been sinfully exalted.

MAIN CHARACTER: Obadiah

OUTLINE

I. Edom's destiny prophesied: 1:1-9

    A. The message is from the Lord to Obadiah regarding Edom: 1:1
    B. Unconquerable Edom will be conquered: 1:2-4
        1. Edom will be small and despised among the nations: 1:2
        2. Deceived by pride: 1:3
        3. Brought down by God: 1:4
    C. Edom will be completely plundered and deserted: 1:5-9
        1. Thieves and robbers: 1:5

- 2. Hidden treasure sought: 1:6
- 4. Edom deceived and trapped: 1:7.
- 5. Wise men destroyed: 1:8
- 6. Mighty men dismayed and Edom cut off: 1:9

II. The cause: 1:10-14

- A. Violence: 1:10
- B. Hostile attitude: 1:11
- C. Joy at the calamity of others: 1:12
- D. Boasting in times of other's distress: 1:12
- E. Spoiling God's people: 1:13
- F. Preventing escape of fugitives: 1:14
- G. Betrayal: 1:14

III. "The day of the Lord" when judgment will come on all heathen nations, not only Edom: 1:15-21

- A. Judgment on Edom and all nations: 1:15-16
    - 1. As you have done, you will receive: 1:15
    - 2. As they have done, they will receive: 1:16
- B. Salvation of the house of Jacob: 1:17-20
    - 1. Deliverance and holiness in Mt. Zion: 1:17
    - 2. Houses of Jacob, Joseph, Esau: 1:18
    - 3. Possessions: 1:19-20
- C. The millennial kingdom of Jesus: 1:21

SELF-TEST

1. Who was the author of the book of Obadiah?

2. State the purpose for the book of Obadiah.

3. To whom was the book of Obadiah written?

4. State the Life and Ministry Principle of the book of Obadiah.

5. Write the Key Verse of Obadiah.

(Answers to tests are provided at the conclusion of the final chapter in this manual.)

FOR FURTHER STUDY

1. For other prophecies against Edom read the following passages:

    -Isaiah 34:5-15
    -Jeremiah 49:7-22
    -Ezekiel 25:12-14; 35:1-5
    -Amos 1:11-12

2. "Edom" means red. The Edomites came from Esau. To read about their history see Genesis 36; Exodus 15:15; Numbers 20:14; 20-21; and Deuteronomy 23:7-8.

3. These are specific sins mentioned in Obadiah in the chapters indicated:

    -Violence: 10
    -Hostile attitude: 11
    -Joy at the calamity of others: 12
    -Boasting in times of other's distress: 12
    -Spoiling God's people: 13
    -Preventing escape of fugitives: 14
    -Betrayal: 14

4. Key phrases in Obadiah:

    -Thus saith the Lord
    -I will
    -Hear this word
    -Thus the Lord showed me

CHAPTER THIRTY-THREE

JONAH

OBJECTIVES:

Upon completion of this chapter you will be able to:

- Name the author of the book of Jonah.
- Identify to whom the book of Jonah was written.
- State the purpose for the book of Jonah.
- Write the Key Verses of the book of Jonah from memory.
- State the Life and Ministry Principle for the book of Jonah.

INTRODUCTION

AUTHOR: Jonah

TO WHOM: The nation of Ninevah to warn of the consequences of disobedience to God.

PURPOSE: The purpose was not only to evangelize Ninevah, but to document for Israel that salvation was not for the Jews only.

KEY VERSES: Jonah 3:1-2

LIFE AND MINISTRY PRINCIPLE: Salvation is not restricted by race, culture, or other barriers: "Whosoever shall call on the name of the Lord shall be saved." (Romans 10:13)

MAIN CHARACTER: Jonah

OUTLINE

I. The first commission: 1:1-2:10

   A. Divine call: Arise, go, cry: 1:1-2
   B. Disobedience of Jonah: He arose and fled: 1:3
   C. Results of disobedience: 1:4-17
      1. Caught in a storm: 1:4-6
      2. Found guilty: 1:7

            3.   Thrown overboard: 1:8-16
            4.   Swallowed by a great fish: 1:17
    D.   Jonah's prayer: 2:1-9
        1.   Remembers the distress of life: 2:3,5-6
        2.   Realizes the direction of God's hand: 2:3
        3.   Recognizes it is the desire of the Lord to answer prayer: 2:2,7
        4.   Requires rededication and repentance: 2:9
        5.   Results in deliverance: 2:10
    E.   Jonah's deliverance: 2:10

II.   The second commission: Arise, go, proclaim: 3:1-10

    A.   Obedience: He arose, went, cried: 3:1-4
    B.   Results of obedience: 3:5-10
        1.   The people believed: 3:5
        2.   They repented: Fasting for man and beast, sackcloth and ashes: 3:5-9
        3.   The city was preserved: 3:10

III.   The prophet's problem: 4:1-11

    A.   The wrath of the prophet: 4:1-5
    B.   The reproof of God: 4:6-11

SELF-TEST

1. Who was the author of the book of Jonah?

   _____

2. State the purpose for the book of Jonah.

   _____

   _____

   _____

3. To whom was the book of Jonah written?

   _____

   _____

4. State the Life and Ministry Principle of the book of Jonah.

   _____

   _____

   _____

5. Write the Key Verses of Jonah.

   _____

   _____

   _____

   _____

(Answers to tests are provided at the conclusion of the final chapter in this manual.)

FOR FURTHER STUDY

1. When God "repented" it did not mean the same as repentance from wrongdoing (3:10). God, in mercy, decided not to send the previously planned judgment because the people of Ninevah believed and acted upon Jonah's message. See Amos 7:3; Luke 11:30; Matthew 12:39.

2. Jonah is a type of the nation of Israel:

    -Chosen to witness: Deuteronomy 14:2; Ezekiel 20:5

    -Commissioned of God: Isaiah 43:10-12 and 44:8

    -Disobedient to the will of the Lord: Exodus 32:1-4; Judges 2:11-19; Ezekiel 6:1-5; Mark 7:6-9

    -Among men of different nationalities: Deuteronomy 4:27; Ezekiel 12:15

    -While among the heathen, they came to know God: Romans 11:11

    -Miraculously preserved: Hosea 3:3; Jeremiah 30:11; 31:35-37

3. Note the reasons Jonah was displeased with God. It was because He was gracious, merciful, slow to anger, great in kindness, and repents of judgment.

4. Jonah was controlled by his emotions. For example, in chapter 4 he was first angry, then glad, then angry again. He was self-willed (chapter 1) and characterized by pride (4:2). He was more concerned with his own happiness and comfort (chapter 4) than lost souls.

5. When running from God, there is . . .

    -Indifference to His commands: 1:2-3
    -Inability to hide from Him: 1:4,17
    -Insecurity in the future: 1:15
    -Incapability of helping self: 1:4-6

6. Jonah is a type of Christ. Both had a special message, Jonah of judgment and Jesus of salvation. Both were in a storm. Jonah was thrown into the water and Jesus calmed the storm. Jonah cried out from the fish and Jesus cried out from the cross. Both rose the third day (Jonah from the fish and Jesus from the tomb) and both preached after their resurrection.

CHAPTER THIRTY-FOUR
MICAH

OBJECTIVES:

Upon completion of this chapter you will be able to:

- Name the author of the book of Micah.
- Identify to whom the book of Micah was written.
- State the purpose for the book of Micah.
- Write the Key Verse of the book of Micah from memory.
- State the Life and Ministry Principle for the book of Micah.

INTRODUCTION

AUTHOR: Micah

TO WHOM: Israel and Judah

PURPOSE: A call to repentance to avoid judgment.

KEY VERSE: Micah 6:8

LIFE AND MINISTRY PRINCIPLE: God judges the oppressors of His people.

MAIN CHARACTER: Micah

OUTLINE

I. Introduction: 1:1

II. General prophecy of judgment: 1:2-2:13

    A. Judgment against Samaria: 1:2-8
        1. Announcement of judgment: 1:2-4
        2. Destruction of Samaria: 1:2-8
    B. Judgment against Judah: 1:9-16

- C. Judgment upon oppressors: 2:1-11
  1. Arrogance and violence of the nobles: 2:1-5
  2. False prophets who would silence the true prophets: 2:6-11
- D. Mercy upon a remnant: 2:12-13

III. The establishment of the Messianic Kingdom: 3:1-5:15

- A. Judgment on wicked rulers, false prophets, and the nations: 3:1-12
  1. Sins of the civil rulers: 3:1-4
  2. Sins of the false prophets: 3:5-8
  3. Rulers, prophets, and priests: 3:9-11
- B. Character of the Kingdom: 4:1-5
- C. Setting up the Kingdom: 4:6-13
  1. Restoration of the former dominion: 4:6-8
  2. Into Babylon before restoration: 4:9-10
  3. Deliverance of Zion and destruction of the enemy: 4:11-5:1
- D. The first advent and rejection of the King: 5:1-2
- E. The interval between the King's rejection and return: 5:3
- F. Events upon His return: 5:4-15
  1. He will provide food for the flock: 5:4
  2. He will be peace of His people: 5:5-6
  3. He will provide power to His people: 5:7-9
     (a) The remnant as dew: 5:7
     (b) The remnant as a lion: 5:8
     (c) The remnant triumphant: 5:9-15

IV. The Lord's problem with His people and His final mercy: 6:1-7:20

- A. The people's ingratitude and wickedness: 6:1-7:6
  1. Ingratitude for blessings: 6:1-5
  2. Righteous conduct is God's requirement, not outward sacrifice: 6:6-8
  3. God's threat of judgment: 6:9-14
- B. The prophet's intercession: 7:7-20
  1. Confession of the nation's guilt: 7:1-6
  2. Confession of faith: 7:7-13
  3. Prayer for renewal of grace: 7:14
  4. The Lord's answer: 7:15-17
  5. Doxology: 7:18-20

SELF-TEST

1. Who was the author of the book of Micah?

2. State the purpose for the book of Micah.

3. To whom was the book of Micah written?

4. State the Life and Ministry Principle of the book of Micah.

5. Write the Key Verse of Micah.

(Answers to tests are provided at the conclusion of the final chapter in this manual.)

FOR FURTHER STUDY

1. A quotation from the book of Micah may have saved the life of Jeremiah the prophet many years later. Read Jeremiah 26:16-18 and compare it to Micah 3:12.

2. Micah 4:1-5 gives one the of the most beautiful descriptions of the millennium in all the Bible.

3. Three words can help you remember the book of Micah:

    -OUTWARD: His public sermons compose chapters 1-6

    -INWARD: His personal thoughts are recorded in 7:1-6

    -UPWARD: His prayer to God is lifted in 7:7-20

4. For the historical background of the kings of Judah mentioned in Micah 1:1 read 2 Kings 15:32-20:21 and 2 Chronicles 27:1-33:20.

5. Micah's prophecy concerns the northern kingdom of Samaria and the southern kingdom of Judah. Each time Samaria is mentioned put NK in the margin. Each time Jerusalem is mentioned put SK in the margin.

6. In Micah 6:6-8 God tells you how to approach Him and what He requires. Study this passage carefully.

CHAPTER THIRTY-FIVE

NAHUM

OBJECTIVES:

Upon completion of this chapter you will be able to:

- Name the author of the book of Nahum.
- Identify to whom the book of Nahum was written.
- State the purpose for the book of Nahum.
- Write the Key Verse of the book of Nahum from memory.
- State the Life and Ministry Principle for the book of Nahum.

INTRODUCTION

AUTHOR: Nahum

TO WHOM: The city of Ninevah.

PURPOSE: To warn of judgment on Ninevah, capitol of the Assyrian empire which took God's people into captivity.

KEY VERSE: Nahum 1:2

LIFE AND MINISTRY PRINCIPLE: Beware, God avenges evil.

MAIN CHARACTER: Nahum

OUTLINE

I. Prophecy of destruction, part one: 1:1-14

    A. Introduction: 1:1
    B. Source of destruction: God Himself: 1:2-9
        1. Vengeance and God's mercy: 1:2-3
        2. His terrible anger against sin: 1:4-6
        3. The greatness of His mercy: 1:7
        4. The pursuer of His enemies: 1:8
    C. Reason for destruction: Sin: 1:9-14

    1. God's faithfulness in the present crisis: 1:9-11
    2. Destruction of Assyria: 1:12-14
    3. Rejoicing in Zion: 1:15

II. Promise to Judah: They no longer need fear this cruel nation: 1:15

III. Prophecy of destruction, part two: 2:1-3:19

  A. The siege and destruction of the city: 2:3-13
    1. Assault upon Ninevah: Doom of the city: 2:1-7
     (a) Furious preparation for battle: 2:1-4
     (b) Hopelessness of resistance: 2:5-6
     (c) The city as a queen is captured: 2:7
    2. Flight of the people and spoiling of the city: 2:8-13
     (a) The inhabitants flee: 2:8-10
     (b) The destruction is complete: 2:11-13
  B. Reasons for Ninevah's fall: 3:1-9
    1. Description of the battle: 3:1-3
    2. The cause: Her sins: 3:1-6,16,19
    3. The uncovering of her shame is of God: 3:5-7
  C. The fate of No-amon is to be the fate of Ninevah: 3:8-11 (See Jeremiah 46:25; Ezekiel 30:14)
  D. Inability of Ninevah to save the city: 3:12-19
    1. Fall of outlying strongholds: 3:12-13
    2. Siege and destructions of the city: 3:14-19a
    3. Universal joy over the fall of Ninevah: 3:19b

SELF-TEST

1. Who was the author of the book of Nahum?

2. State the purpose for the book of Nahum.

3. To whom was the book of Nahum written?

4. State the Life and Ministry Principle of the book of Nahum.

5. Write the Key Verse of Nahum.

(Answers to tests are provided at the conclusion of the final chapter in this manual.)

FOR FURTHER STUDY

1. List the reasons for God's judgment of Ninevah.

2. Do you remember the other prophet you previously studied, who also prophesied to Ninevah? How did the city respond to this earlier prophecy? (See the book of Jonah).

3. Compare these verses:

    Isaiah 8:8; 10:23   Nahum 1:8-9
    Isaiah 24:1   Nahum 2:10
    Isaiah 21:3   Nahum 2:10
    Isaiah 52:7   Nahum 1:15

4. Here are some of the reasons for Ninevah's fall:

    -Bloodshed: 3:1
    -Lies: 3:1
    -Robbery: 3:1
    -Killing of the innocent: 3:3-4
    -Whoredom: 3:4
    -Witchcraft: 3:4
    -Immorality: 3:5
    -Hidden violence: 3:6
    -Merchants (hired soldiers) who destroy: 3:16
    -A wound so bad it could not be healed: 3:19
    -Continual wickedness: 3:19

CHAPTER THIRTY-SIX

HABAKKUK

OBJECTIVES:

Upon completion of this chapter you will be able to:

- Name the author of the book of Habakkuk.
- Identify to whom the book of Habakkuk was written.
- State the purpose for the book of Habakkuk.
- Write the Key Verse of the book of Habakkuk from memory.
- State the Life and Ministry Principle for the book of Habakkuk.

INTRODUCTION

AUTHOR: Habakkuk

TO WHOM: Judah

PURPOSE: Awaken Judah to their spiritual needs and warn of impending judgment from God.

KEY VERSE: Habakkuk 3:2

LIFE AND MINISTRY PRINCIPLE: The just shall live by faith.

MAIN CHARACTER: Habakkuk

OUTLINE

This book divides easily into three sections according to chapters. Habakkuk records a spiritual burden (chapter 1), a vision (chapter 2), and a prayer (chapter 3), all of which relate to the judgment of Judah by God through the Chaldean nation.

I. Topic sentence: 1:1

II. Habakkuk's first complaint: 1:2-4

    A. The prophet's questions: 1:2-3a
    B. The moral and civil conditions of Judah: 1:3b
    C. The prophet's conclusions: 1:4

III. The Lord's reply: 1:5-11

   A. The marvelous work announced: 1:5
   B. The Chaldeans and their might: 1:6-11

IV. Habakkuk's confidence in the Lord: 1:12

V. Habakkuk's second complaint: 1:13-17

VI. The waiting prophet: 2:1

VII. The Lord's answer: 2:2-4

   A. The vision to be written plainly: 2:2
   B. The vision surely to come: 2:3
   C. The vision: 2:4

VIII. The five woes: 23:5-19

   A. Introduction: 2:5-6a
   B. The five woes upon the Chaldeans: 2:6b-19
      1. The first woe: 2:6b-8
      2. The second woe: 2:9-11
      3. The third woe: 2:12-13
   (Earth filled with the knowledge of the Lord: 2:14)
      4. The fourth woe: 2:15-18
      5. The fifth woe: 2:19

IX. Habakkuk's psalm: 3:1-19

   A. The title: 2:1
   B. The plea: 3:2
   C. The Lord's answer: 3:3-15
   D. Habakkuk's response: 3:16-19a
   E. The musical ascription: 3:19b

SELF-TEST

1. Who was the author of the book of Habakkuk?

2. State the purpose for the book of Habakkuk.

3. To whom was the book of Habakkuk written?

4. State the Life and Ministry Principle of the book of Habakkuk.

5. Write the Key Verse of Habakkuk.

(Answers to tests are provided at the conclusion of the final chapter in this manual.)

FOR FURTHER STUDY

1. Habakkuk's statement, "the just shall live by faith," is quoted three times in the New Testament. See Romans 1:17, Galatians 3:11, and Hebrews 10:38.

2. See also Acts 13:40-41 and Philippians 4:4, 10-19.

3. An "oracle" can be translated "a burden." What is Habakkuk's burden? What is bothering him?

4. Mark each reference to God, the Holy One, Lord, and every personal pronoun which refers to God. Summarize what you learn about God from this book.

5. Mark the references to the "proud or haughty man." Summarize what he is like and with whom he is contrasted. James 4 indicates that God resists the proud.

6. Mark each use of the word "woe" and then observe to whom the woe is going to come, why it will come, and what will happen when it comes. Would any of these be applicable to you because of your lifestyle? If so, repent.

CHAPTER THIRTY-SEVEN

ZEPHANIAH

OBJECTIVES:

Upon completion of this chapter you will be able to:

- Name the author of the book of Zephaniah.
- Identify to whom the book of Zephaniah was written.
- State the purpose for the book of Zephaniah.
- Write the Key Verse of the book of Zephaniah from memory.
- State the Life and Ministry Principle for the book of Zephaniah.

INTRODUCTION

AUTHOR: Zephaniah

TO WHOM: Israel

PURPOSE: To warn Israel and all nations of the judgment of God.

KEY VERSE: Zephaniah 3:17

LIFE AND MINISTRY PRINCIPLE: God is mighty to save.

MAIN CHARACTER: Zephaniah

OUTLINE

I. Introduction: 1:1-3

    A. The messenger: 1:1
    B. Summary of the message: 1:2-3

II. A look within: 1:4-2:3

    A. The fact of judgment: 1:4-14
        1. Judgment on four kinds of worshipers: 1:4-7
        2. Judgment on sinners of every rank: 1:8-13

- B. The nature and results of judgment: 1:14-18
    1. It is at hand: 1:14
    2. Even the mighty are brought low: 1:14
    3. Dark day of distress, waste, desolation: 1:15-16
    4. Distress, blood, flesh as dung: 1:17
    5. No deliverance: 1:18
    6. Day of the Lord's anger: 1:2-3
- C. The name of judgment: Day of the Lord: 2:1-3
- D. Hope in judgment: 2:3

III. A look around: Judgment coming on all nations: 2:4-3:7

- A. Philistine cities: 2:4-7
- B. Moab and Ammon: 2:8-11
- C. Ethiopia: 2:12
- D. Assyria and its capitol, Ninevah: 2:13-15
- E. Judgment on Jerusalem: 3:1-7
    1. Note the condition of Jerusalem:
        (a) Filthy, oppressing, polluted: 3:1
        (b) Disobedient: 3:2
        (c) Evil secular leaders: 3:3
        (d) Evil spiritual leaders: 3:4
    2. Note the mercies of God: 3:5-7

IV. A look beyond: After judgment, healing will come: 3:8-20
- A. God's purpose accomplished: 3:8
- B. From among the heathen, God's remnant will come: 3:9-10, 12-13
- C. Judgment on those who were once enemies of God: 3:9-13
- D. Israel's Messiah manifested as King: 3:14-20

SELF-TEST

1. Who was the author of the book of Zephaniah?

   _____

2. State the purpose for the book of Zephaniah.

   _____

   _____

   _____

3. To whom was the book of Zephaniah written?

   _____

   _____

4. State the Life and Ministry Principle of the book of Zephaniah.

   _____

   _____

   _____

5. Write the Key Verse of Zephaniah.

   _____

   _____

   _____

(Answers to tests are provided at the conclusion of the final chapter in this manual.)

FOR FURTHER STUDY

1. The title "the King of Israel" is used for God only twice in the Bible. Zephaniah uses it in the Old Testament (3:15). Nathaniel, a disciple of Jesus, used it in the New Testament (John 1:49).

2. Zephaniah calls the judgment he describes "the day of the Lord." He uses this title seven times. (See 1:7,8,14,18; 2:2-3.)

   This is what we learn about the day of the Lord:

   -It is at hand: 1:4,7,14
   -Even the mighty will be brought low: 1:14
   -It is a time of darkness, terror, wrath, desolation: 1:15
   -It is a time of alarm: 1:16
   -Judgment will come upon sin: 1:17
   -It will be accompanied by great signs in nature: 1:15
   -It is the day of the Lord's anger: 1:2-3
   -It falls upon all creation: 2:1-15; 3:8

CHAPTER THIRTY-EIGHT

HAGGAI

OBJECTIVES:

Upon completion of this chapter you will be able to:

- Name the author of the book of Haggai.
- Identify to whom the book of Haggai was written.
- State the purpose for the book of Haggai.
- Write the Key Verse of the book of Haggai from memory.
- State the Life and Ministry Principle for the book of Haggai.

INTRODUCTION

AUTHOR: Haggai

TO WHOM: Israel, after the exile; particularly the Jews who had returned to Jerusalem.

PURPOSE: To inspire Israel to new zeal for God and make the leaders aware of their responsibility to rebuild the temple of worship.

KEY VERSE: Haggai 1:5

LIFE AND MINISTRY PRINCIPLE: Building God's Kingdom should be a priority of the true believer.

MAIN CHARACTER: Haggai

OUTLINE

I. First message: A summons to rebuild the temple (given on the first day of the sixth month) 1:1-15

    A. The date: 1:1
    B. The message: 1:2-11
        1. The people's procrastination: 1:2-4
        2. It's consequences: 1:5-11
    C. The people's response: 1:12-15
        1. Obedience and fear of the Lord: 1:12

        2.   The work of encouragement: 1:13
        3.   The work begun: 1:14
        4.   The date: 1:15

II.   Second message: Prophecy of the Millennial temple which would be greater than the temple they would now build (given the 21st day of the seventh month) 2:1-9

    A.   The date: 2:1
    B.   The message: 2:2-9
        1.   The temples compared: 2:2-3
        2.   The answer to discouragement: 2:4-5
        3.   The universal shaking and later glory of the temple: 2:6-9

III.   Third message: Promise of present blessing on the rebuilding of the temple (given the 24th day of the ninth month) 2:10-19

    A.   The date: 2:10
    B.   The message: Sin is contagious: 2:11-19
        1.   The priests questioned: 2:11-13
        2.   The application: 2:14-19

IV.   Fourth message: Prophecy of future destruction of Gentile world powers (given the 24th day of the ninth month) 2:20-23

    A.   The date: 2:20
    B.   The message: 2:21-23
        1.   Overthrow of earthly power: 2:21-22
        2.   Zerubbabel the signet: 2:23

SELF-TEST

1. Who was the author of the book of Haggai?

   _____

2. State the purpose for the book of Haggai.

   _____

   _____

3. To whom was the book of Haggai written?

   _____

   _____

4. State the Life and Ministry Principle of the book of Haggai.

   _____

   _____

   _____

5. Write the Key Verse of Haggai.

   _____

   _____

   _____

(Answers to tests are provided at the conclusion of the final chapter in this manual.)

FOR FURTHER STUDY

1. Read Haggai 1:9 to find the reasons Israel was not being blessed by God.

2. Spiritual truths in Haggai:

    -The Lord's work takes priority over all.

    -The Lord's work demands clean instruments.

    -The Lord's work is linked to God's plan for all nations.

    -Good is not contagious, but evil is.

3. You are the temple of the Holy Spirit. Apply the truths of Haggai to yourself personally. Have you given too much attention and time to your personal affairs and neglected the things of God that are important for spreading the Gospel and the furtherance of His work?

4. Mark every reference to "the word of the Lord came by the prophet Haggai" and "the word of the Lord came by Haggai the prophet." Each occurrence of these phrases begins a message. It will help you see the structure of Haggai.

5. For the historical setting of Haggai read Ezra 4:24-6:22.

6. God told Israel, "I will make thee as a signet" (Haggai 2:23). A signet ring was often a seal of a pledge. It was also used as a mark of honor and a badge of royal authority. Christ was God's "signet" with which He imprinted upon all believers His image and delegated to us His authority.

7. Apply the teachings of Haggai about work to the unfinished task of the church of reaching the world with the gospel. Think about these things:

    -This work should take priority over other obligations.
    -This mission demands clean instruments.
    -The task is linked to God's plan for men and nations.

8. If Haggai was writing to you personally in terms of how you are fulfilling the Great Commission, what do you think he would say?

CHAPTER THIRTY-NINE

ZECHARIAH

OBJECTIVES:

Upon completion of this chapter you will be able to:

- Name the author of the book of Zechariah.
- Identify to whom the book of Zechariah was written.
- State the purpose for the book of Zechariah.
- Write the Key Verse of the book of Zechariah from memory.
- State the Life and Ministry Principle for the book of Zechariah.

INTRODUCTION

AUTHOR: Zechariah

TO WHOM: Israel

PURPOSE: To inspire Israel to finish the temple.

KEY VERSE: Zechariah 13:1

LIFE AND MINISTRY PRINCIPLE: God controls the affairs of men and nations.

MAIN CHARACTER: Zechariah

OUTLINE

I. Introductory call to repentance: 1:1-6

II. Prophecies by vision: 1:7-6:8

    A. The man among the myrtle trees: 1:7-17
       (Israel outcast, but not forgotten by God.)
    B. The four horns: 1:18-21
       (The overthrow of Israel by her enemies.)
    C. The man with the measuring rod: 2:1-13
       (The coming prosperity of Jerusalem.)

- D. Joshua the high priest: 3:1-10
  (Israel's sin removed by Jesus, the Branch.)
- E. The candlestick and the two trees: 4:1-14
  (Israel is God's future light-bearer.)
  1. The first question and explanation: 4:1-10
  2. The second question and explanation: 4:11-14
- F. The flying roll: 5:1-4
  (Wicked governments cursed by God)
- G. The woman in the ephah: 5:5-11
  (Wickedness removed on divine wings)
- H. The four chariots: 6:1-8
  (God's judgments.)

III. Illustrative prophecies: 6:9-8:23

- A. The returning Jews: 6:9-15
- B. Vanities of the people: 7:1-8:23
  1. Fast days of Israel and obedience to the Word: 7:1-17
     - (a) Occasion of the prophecy: 7:1-3
     - (b) Fasting not essential, but hearing is: 7:4-7
  2. First half of the Lord's answer to the question of fasting: 7:8-14
     - (a) What God requires of the fathers: 7:8-10
     - (b) Refusal of the fathers to hearken: 7:11-14
  3. The second half of the Lord's answer: 8:1-23
     - (a) The time of redemption: 8:1-8
     - (b) Message of encouragement: 8:9-17
     - (c) Fasting to be changed to rejoicing: 8:18-23

IV. Direct prophecies: 9:1-14:21
- A. The first prophecy: The first coming and rejection of Jesus: 9:1-11:17
  1. Fall of the heathen world and deliverance of Zion: 9-10
  2. Good and foolish shepherds: 11:1-17
     - (a) The humiliated land: 11:1-3
     - (b) The good shepherd: 11:4-14
     - (c) The foolish shepherd: 11:15-17
- B. The second prophecy: The second coming and acceptance of Jesus: 12:1-14:21
  1. Future deliverance and conversion of Israel: 12:1-13:9
     - (a) Deliverance of Judah and Jerusalem: 12:1-9
     - (b) Spirit of grace and lamentation: 12:10-14
     - (c) A fountain of grace for salvation: 13:1-6
  2. The return of Jesus: 14:1-21
     - (a) Judgment and deliverance: 14:1-5
     - (b) Complete salvation: 14:6-11

(c) Destruction of enemy nations: 14:12-15
(d) Conversion of heathen nations: 14:16-19
(e) Everything unholy removed: 14:20-21

SELF-TEST

1. Who was the author of the book of Zechariah?

   _____

2. State the purpose for the book of Zechariah.

   _____

   _____

   _____

3. To whom was the book of Zechariah written?

   _____

   _____

4. State the Life and Ministry Principle of the book of Zechariah.

   _____

   _____

   _____

5. Write the Key Verse of Zechariah.

   _____

   _____

   _____

(Answers to tests are provided at the conclusion of the final chapter in this manual.)

FOR FURTHER STUDY

1. The book of Zechariah provides much information on the ministry of angels. See chapters 1 and 2.

2. Like the book of Job, Zechariah offers a glimpse into heaven to view the confrontations between God and Satan. See Job 1 and 2 and Zechariah 3:1-5.

3. Several facts about Jesus are presented in Zechariah:

    -His commission: 2:8-11
    -His present work: 3:1-2
    -His concern over Jerusalem: 1:12
    -His title: 6:12
    -His temple: 6:13
    -His triumphal entry to Jerusalem: 9:9
    -His betrayal: 11:12
    -His crucifixion: 12:10; 13:7
    -His final recognition by Israel: 12:1
    -His appearance on Mt Zion: 14:4
    -His worship by all nations: 14:16
    -His victory at Armageddon: 14:3

4. Several facts about the city of God are presented in Zechariah:

    -A city of truth: 8:3
    -Surrounded by God's glory: 2:5
    -Filled with children: 8:5
    -Visited by all nations: 8:20-23
    -Once again besieged by enemies: 12:2; 14:2
    -Its enemies are destroyed: 12:9; 14:12-14
    -Its citizens recognize the Messiah: 12:10
    -Filled with God's holiness: 14:21

CHAPTER FORTY

MALACHI

OBJECTIVES:

Upon completion of this chapter you will be able to:

- Name the author of the book of Malachi.
- Identify to whom the book of Malachi was written.
- State the purpose for the book of Malachi.
- Write the Key Verse of the book of Malachi from memory.
- State the Life and Ministry Principle for the book of Malachi.

INTRODUCTION

AUTHOR: Malachi

TO WHOM: Israel

PURPOSE: To call the nation to repentance and return to righteousness.

KEY VERSE: Malachi 2:2

LIFE AND MINISTRY PRINCIPLE:

Repentance (attitude) + Returning (action) = Restoration

Both attitude (repentance from sin) and action (returning to God) are necessary for forgiveness (restoration to righteousness before God).

MAIN CHARACTER: Malachi

OUTLINE

I. Introduction: 1:1-5

    A. The messenger: 1:1
    B. The message: 1:1
    C. The recipient of the message: Israel: 1:1
    D. God's love for Israel: 1:2-5

                1.   Essau and Jacob: 1:2-3
                2.   God and Edom: 1:4-5

II.   A message to the priests: 1:6-2:9

        A.   Their neglect in religious duties: 1:6-2:4
              1.   Worthlessness of sacrifices: 1:6-14
              2.   Better to shut the temple than engage in worthless worship: 1:9-10
              3.   Superior service among the Gentiles: 1:11
              4.   Weariness in worship: 1:12-13 contrasted with wonderful worship in 1:11.
              5.   The curse of God: 1:14-2:4
        B.   Their faulty teaching of the law: 2:5-9
              1.   Covenant with Levi and the ideal priest: 2:5-7
              2.   The apostate priests and their disgrace: 2:8-9

III.   A message to the Jewish laymen: 2:10-4:3

        A.   A charge of treachery: 2:10-16
        B.   Warning of judgment: 2:17-3:6
              1.   Their questions: 2:17
              2.   God's refining fire: 3:1-3
              3.   Purification of the priest and people: 3:3-5
              4.   God does not change: 3:6
        C.   A call to repentance: 3:7-12
              1.   The people's unfaithfulness and God's curse: 3:7-9
              2.   God's reward for their respect and faithfulness: 3:10-12
        D.   Divine indictment for sin: 3:13-4:3
              1.   Complaint: 3:13-15
              2.   Separation of the righteous from the wicked: 3:16-18
              3.   Utter destruction of the wicked: 4:1
              4.   Exaltation and glorification of the righteous: 4:2-3

IV.   Concluding warning: 4:4-6

        A.   Keep the law of Moses: 4:4
        B.   Look for the second coming of Jesus: 4:5-6

SELF-TEST

1. Who was the author of the book of Malachi?

   _____

2. State the purpose for the book of Malachi.

   _____

   _____

   _____

3. To whom was the book of Malachi written?

   _____

   _____

4. State the Life and Ministry Principle of the book of Malachi.

   _____

   _____

   _____

5. Write the Key Verse of Malachi.

   _____

   _____

   _____

(Answers to tests are provided at the conclusion of the final chapter in this manual.)

FOR FURTHER STUDY

1. Malachi contains several key passages:

   -The most famous Old Testament passage on giving: 3:8-10

   -The most wonderful diary of all time: 3:16

   -The only passage in which believers are called Jewels: 3:17

   -The only Old Testament book predicting Elijah's return to minister during the tribulation: 4:15

2. It is difficult for man to accept the fact he has sinned. Note how the people argued with God's judgment in the book of Malachi. "Wherein" is the key word which precedes each argument of the people: 1:2,6,7; 2:17; 3:7,8,13

3. Note the minister's chief areas of temptation: 1:6-2:9

4. There are several "beholds" to note in this book:

   -Behold I will corrupt and reject worship: 2:3
   -Behold I will send my messenger (John the Baptist): 3:1
   -Behold the earth will burn: 4:1
   -Behold Elijah will warn: 4:5

5. "God's Book Of Remembrance": See also Exodus 32:32; Psalms 56:8; 69:28; 139:16; Ezekiel 13:9; Daniel 7:10; 11:1; Philippians 4:3; Revelation 20:12

6. Although most of the prophets lived and prophesied in days of change and political upheaval, Malachi lived in an uneventful waiting period when God seemed to have forgotten His people who were enduring poverty and foreign domination in Judah. The day of miracles seemed to have passed with Elijah and Elisha. The Temple was not completed and nothing profound had occurred to indicate God's presence had returned to fill it with glory as Ezekiel prophesied (Ezekiel 43:4). The people continued their religious duties without enthusiasm. In reality, the promises that had been given were conditional and the people were not meeting the requirements of God to enable them to receive them. Malachi's prophecy permits us to see the strains and temptations of the waiting periods of life. More important, he also shows the way back to genuine faith in the God who does not change (3:6); who invites men to return to Him (3:7); and who never forgets those who respond (3:16).

ANSWERS TO SELF-TESTS

CHAPTER ONE:

1. All Scripture is given by inspiration of God, and is profitable for doctrine, for reproof, for correction, for instruction in righteousness:

   That the man of God may be perfect, thoroughly furnished unto all good works. (II Timothy 4:16-17)

2. The word "Bible" means "the books."

3. The word "Scripture" means "sacred writings."

4. Old Testament and New Testament.

5. 66.

6. Law, history, poetry, prophecy.

7. Gospels, history, letters, prophecy.

8. The word "testament" means "covenant."

9. For doctrine, reproof, correction, instruction in righteousness. (II Timothy 3:16-17)

10. The Bible contains no contradictions and is united in its major theme.

11. The Bible has variety.

12. a. T; b. T; c. F; d. F; e. F

13. Jesus. Luke 24:44-48.

CHAPTER TWO:

1. Let my cry come near before thee, O Lord; give me understanding according to thy Word. (Psalms 119:169)

2. 39

3. 27

4. You must read it systematically if you are to understand its content.

5. Read daily, read selectively, read prayerfully, read systematically.

CHAPTER THREE:

1. The Lord gave the word: great was the company of those that published it. (Psalms 68:11)

2. A version is a Bible written in a language different from the languages in which God's Word was originally written.

3. A translation is a word by word translation of the Greek, Hebrew, and Aramaic words. A paraphrase does not translate word for word. It is translated thought by thought.

4. The King James version.

5. Because no two languages are exactly alike, so differences occur when translation is done.

6. Hebrew, Aramaic, and Greek.

CHAPTER FOUR:

1. Moreover He said unto me, Son of man, all my words that I shall speak unto thee receive in thine heart and hear with thine ears. (Ezekiel 3:8)

2. An outline is a method of organizing study notes. It puts information in summary for future use in ministry and study.

3. If you have difficulty understanding the outline, review the instructions for outlining given in this chapter.

4. Main points are indicated on an outline by a Roman numeral.

5. Subpoints under a main point are indicated by a capital letter of the alphabet.

CHAPTER FIVE:

1. Moses.

2. To preserve the historical background of Israel and the record of creation, sin, redemption, and God's first dealings with man.

3. Israel.

4. God's plan from the beginning included all nations. God begins new things with people.

5. And I will put enmity between thee and the woman, and between thy seed and her seed; it shall bruise thy head, and thou shalt bruise his heel. (Genesis 3:15)

CHAPTER SIX:

1. Moses.

2. To record the deliverance of Israel from slavery and document their purpose for existence as a nation.

3. Israel.

4. Salvation comes only through the blood of the Lamb of God, Jesus.

5. And the blood shall be to you for a token upon the houses where ye are: and when I see the blood, I will pass over you, and the plague shall not be upon you to destroy you, when I smite the land of Egypt. (Exodus 12:13)

CHAPTER SEVEN:

1. Moses.

2. To show Israel how to live as a holy nation in fellowship with God and prepare them to extend the redemptive plan of God to all nations.

3. Israel.

4. God requires holiness of His people.

5. Sanctify yourselves therefore, and be ye holy: for I am the Lord your God. (Leviticus 20:7)

CHAPTER EIGHT:

1. Moses.

2. Records experiences of the wilderness journey which are a type of the defeated Christian.

3. Israel.

4. God is not pleased with anything less than total commitment.

5. But if ye will not do so, behold, ye have sinned against the Lord; and be sure your sin will find you out. (Numbers 32:23)

CHAPTER NINE:

1. Moses.

2. To restate the law to the new generations of Israel which had been born since Mt. Sinai.

3. Israel.

4. Obedience brings blessing. Disobedience brings judgment.

5. Hear, O Israel: The Lord our God is one Lord: And thou shalt love the Lord thy God with all thine heart, and with all thy soul, and with all thy might. (Deuteronomy 6:4-5)

CHAPTER TEN:

1. Joshua.

2. Record the history of the conquest of Canaan.

3. Israel.

4. No moral or spiritual victories are won without battles.

5. And if it seem evil unto you to serve the Lord, choose you this day whom ye will serve; whether the gods which your fathers served that were on the other side of the flood, or the gods of the Amorites in whose land ye dwell; but as for me and my house, we will serve the Lord. (Joshua 24:15)

CHAPTER ELEVEN:

1. Samuel.

2. Historical record of the rule of the judges which occurred after the close of the book of Joshua.

3. Israel.

4. There is a divine pattern of chastisement designed to turn God's people from sin to salvation.

5. In those days there was no king in Israel, but every man did that which was right in his own eyes. (Judges 17:6)

CHAPTER TWELVE:

1. The author is unknown.

2. Written as part of the historical record of Israel to illustrate the concern of God for all people. It also illustrates the kinsman-redeemer relationship of Jesus Christ.

3. Israel.

4. God can turn bitterness to blessing.

5. And Ruth said, Entreat me not to leave thee, or to return from following after thee: for whither thou goest, I will go: and where thou lodgest, I will lodge: thy people shall be my people, and thy God my God:

   Where thou diest will I die, and there will I be buried: the Lord do so to me, and more also, if ought but death part thee and me. (Ruth 1:16-17)

CHAPTER THIRTEEN:

1. Samuel.

2. To continue the record of God's dealing with His people.

3. Israel.

4. Obedience to God is more important than sacrifice.

5. And Samuel said, Hath the Lord as great delight in burnt offerings and sacrifices as in obeying the voice of the Lord? Behold, to obey is better than sacrifice and to hearken than the fat of rams.

   For rebellion is as the sin of witchcraft and stubbornness is as iniquity and idolatry. Because thou hast rejected the word of the Lord, he hath also rejected thee from being king. (I Samuel 15:22-23)

6. Continue the historical record of God's dealing with His people.

7. Israel.

8. God carries out His plan through those obedient to Him in spite of their human frailties.

9. Wherefore thou art great, O Lord God: for there is none like thee, neither is there any God beside thee, according to all that we have heard with our ears.

   And what one nation in the earth is like thy people, even like Israel, whom God went to redeem for a people to Himself and to make Him a name, and to do for you things great and terrible, for thy land, before thy people, which thou redeemedst to thee from Egypt, from the nations and their gods. (II Samuel 7:22-23)

CHAPTER FOURTEEN:

1. The author is unknown. It was possibly Jeremiah.

2. To continue the record of God's dealings with His people, Israel.

3. Israel.

4. Compromise may seem an easy way but it is always costly later.

5. Yet I have left me seven thousand in Israel, all the knees which have not bowed unto Baal, and every mouth which hath not kissed him. (I Kings 19:18)

6. To continue the record of God's dealings with His people, Israel.

7. Israel.

8. Kingdoms of this world are temporal: They rise and fall under God's control.

9. And it came to pass, when they were gone over, that Elijah said unto Elisha, Ask what I shall do for thee, before I be taken away from thee. And Elisha said, I pray thee, let a double portion of thy spirit be upon me.

And he said, Thou hast asked a hard thing: nevertheless, if thou see me when I am taken from thee, it shall be so unto thee; but if not, it shall not be so. (II Kings 2:9-10)

CHAPTER FIFTEEN:

1. The author is unknown. It was possibly Ezra.

2. To record the religious history of Judah.

3. Israel.

4. When God is exalted, His people are blessed.

5. Thine, O Lord, is the greatness, and the power, and the glory, and the victory, and the majesty: for all that is in the heaven and in the earth is thine; thine is the kingdom, O Lord, and thou art exalted as head above all. (I Chronicles 29:11)

6. To record the religious history of Judah.

7. Israel.

8. God's blessing comes by humbling ourselves and seeking Him.

9. If my people, which are called by my name, shall humble themselves, and pray, and seek my face, and turn from their wicked ways; then will I hear from heaven, and will forgive their sin, and will heal their land. (II Chronicles 7:14)

CHAPTER SIXTEEN:

1. Ezra.

2. Ezra tells of the return of God's people from exile in Babylon and the rebuilding of the temple in Jerusalem.

3. Israel.

4. Return and restoration are basic principles of repentance.

5. And the children of Israel, the priests, and the Levites and the rest of the children of the captivity, kept the dedication of this house of God with joy. (Ezra 6:16)

CHAPTER SEVENTEEN:

1. Nehemiah.

2. Continuation of the history of Israel. Record of the rebuilding of the walls of Jerusalem.

3. Israel.

4. There is no opportunity without opposition Faith without works is dead.

5. And I sent messengers unto them saying, I am doing a great work, so that I cannot come down: why should the work cease, whilst I leave it, and come down to you? (Nehemiah 6:3)

CHAPTER EIGHTEEN:

1. Unknown.

2. Continuation of history of Israel. Also to recount the providential care of God for His people.

3. Jews scattered throughout Persia.

4. God meets the crises of life with human vessels which He has prepared.

5. For if thou altogether holdest thy peace at this time, then shall there enlargement and deliverance arise to the Jews from another place; but thou and thy father's house shall be destroyed: and who knoweth whether thou art come to the kingdom for such a time as this? (Esther 4:14)

CHAPTER NINETEEN:

1. Unknown.

2. This book wrestles with the question, "Why do the righteous suffer?"

3. The book is not specifically addressed to anyone but is applicable to all believers who experience suffering.

4. There is a spiritual reason behind suffering of the righteous. Suffering is not necessarily evidence of the displeasure of God.

5. For I know that my redeemer liveth, and that He shall stand at the latter day upon the earth. And thou after my skin worms destroy this body, yet in my flesh shall I see God: Whom I shall see for myself, and mine eyes shall behold, and not another; though my reins be consumed within me. (Job 19:25-27)

   But He knoweth the way that I take: when He hath tried me, I shall come forth as gold. (Job 23:10)

CHAPTER TWENTY:

1. King David was the author of most of the Psalms.

2. The book of Psalms was known as the hymn book of Israel. It is the prayer and praise book of the Bible.

3. Israel, but the book has been used for devotion, prayer, and praise by believers down through the centuries.

4. Prayer, praise, intercession, and confession are all part of true worship.

5. O Come, let us sing unto the Lord; let us make a joyful noise to the rock of our salvation. (Psalms 95:1)

CHAPTER TWENTY-ONE:

1. Solomon.

2. These are listed in Proverbs 1:1-6.

3. Israel, but the truths for practical living are applicable to all believers.

4. Vertical wisdom is necessary for horizontal living. Proverbs is a collection of wise principles given by God to man (vertical) to govern living with others (horizontal).

5. Happy is the man that findeth wisdom, and the man that getteth understanding. (Proverbs 3:13)

CHAPTER TWENTY-TWO:

1. Solomon.

2. A description of the search for life apart from God.

3. Israel and believers in general with a special emphasis towards youth.

4. Life apart from God is futile.

5. Let us hear the conclusion of the whole matter: Fear God and keep His commandments: for this is the whole duty of man. (Ecclesiastes 12:13)

CHAPTER TWENTY-THREE:

1. Solomon.

2. To show the relationship between Jesus and the Church as demonstrated by the marriage relationship.

3. Israel and all believers.

4. The divine model of love between a man and his wife is the pattern for relationship between Christ and the Church.

5. Many waters cannot quench love, neither can the floods drown it: if a man would give all the substance of his house for love, it would utterly be contemned. (Song of Solomon 8:7)

CHAPTER TWENTY-FOUR:

1. Isaiah.

2. Correction and reproof.

3. Judah.

4. Rebellion leads to retribution. Repentance leads to restoration.

5. All we like sheep have gone astray; we have turned every one to his own way; and the Lord hath laid on Him the iniquity of us all. (Isaiah 53:6)

CHAPTER TWENTY-FIVE:

1. Jeremiah.

2. To warn of the coming judgment of captivity and call for repentance.

3. Judah.

4. National disasters and deteriorations are often due to disobedience to God.

5. Call unto me, and I will answer thee, and shew thee great and mighty things, which thou knowest not. (Jeremiah 33:3)

   But the Lord said unto me, Say not, I am a child: for thou shalt go to all that I shall send thee, and whatsoever I command thee thou shalt speak. Be not afraid of their faces: for I am with thee to deliver thee, saith the Lord. (Jeremiah 1:7-8)

CHAPTER TWENTY-SIX:

1. Jeremiah.

2. To produce repentance necessary for spiritual restoration.

3. Jews who were captive in Babylon.

4. God is faithful in both judgment and mercy.

5. It is of the Lord's mercies that we are not consumed, because His compassions fail not. They are new every morning: great is thy faithfulness. (Lamentations 3:22-23)

CHAPTER TWENTY-SEVEN:

1. Ezekiel.

2. Ezekiel warned of the coming captivity, then prophesied to the captives after it occurred.
3. Judah.

4. The Lord orders historical events so that the nations will know He is God.

5. And I sought for a man among them, that should make up the hedge, and stand in the gap before me for the land, that I should not destroy it: but I found none. (Ezekiel 22:30)

CHAPTER TWENTY-EIGHT:

1. Daniel.

2. To show how God rules the affairs of men.

3. Jewish captives.

4. God is sovereign and He honors those who honor Him.

5. And they that be wise shall shine as the brightness of the firmament; and they that turn many to righteousness as the stars for ever and ever. (Daniel 12:3)

CHAPTER TWENTY-NINE:

1. Hosea.

2. To alert Israel to her sinful condition and bring her back to God.

3. The northern kingdom of Israel.

4. Personal experience fosters genuine understanding and compassion.

5. Hear the Word of the Lord. . . for the Lord hath a controversy with the inhabitants of the land, because there is no truth, nor mercy, nor knowledge of God in the land. (Hosea 4:1)

CHAPTER THIRTY:

1. Joel.

2. To warn Judah of their sin and need for repentance and inform of God's future plans for the nation.

3. Judah.

4. Even in the midst of corrective judgment, God plans future blessing for His people.

5. And it shall come to pass afterward, that I will pour out my spirit upon all flesh; and your sons and your daughters shall prophesy, your old men shall dream dreams, your young men shall see visions: And also upon the servants and upon the handmaids in those days will I pour out my spirit. (Joel 2:28-29)

CHAPTER THIRTY-ONE:

1. Amos.

2. To call Israel back to God.

3. Israel.

4. The call to the nations today is still "Prepare to meet thy God."

5. Therefore thus will I do unto thee, O Israel: and because I will do this unto thee, prepare to meet thy God, O Israel. (Amos 4:12)

CHAPTER THIRTY-TWO:

1. Obadiah.

2. To warn of God's punishment for sin.

3. Edom.

4. God brings down that which has been sinfully exalted.

5. Though thou exalt thyself as the eagle, and though thou set thy nest among the stars, thence will I bring thee down, saith the Lord. (Obadiah 1:4)

CHAPTER THIRTY-THREE:

1. Jonah.

2. The purpose was not only to evangelize Ninevah, but to document for Israel that salvation was not for the Jews only.

3. Ninevah.

4. Salvation is not restricted by race, culture, or other barriers. See Romans 10:13.

5. And the word of the Lord came unto Jonah the second time, saying, Arise, go unto Ninevah, that great city, and preach unto it the preaching that I bid thee. (Jonah 3:1-2)

CHAPTER THIRTY-FOUR:

1. Micah.

2. A call to repentance to avoid judgment.

3. Israel and Judah.

4. God judges the oppressors of His people.

5. He hath shewed thee, O man, what is good; and what doth the Lord require of thee, but to do justly, and to love mercy, and to walk humbly with thy God? (Micah 6:8)

CHAPTER THIRTY-FIVE:

1. Nahum.

2. To warn of judgment on Ninevah, capitol of the Assyrian empire which took God's people into captivity.

3. Ninevah.

4. Beware, God avenges evil.

5. God is jealous, and the Lord revengeth; the Lord revengeth, and is furious; the Lord will take vengeance on His adversaries, and He reserveth wrath for His enemies. (Nahum 1:2)

CHAPTER THIRTY-SIX:

1. Habakkuk.

2. To awaken Judah to their spiritual need and warn of impending judgment from God.

3. Judah.

4. The just shall live by faith.

5. O Lord, I have heard thy speech, and was afraid: O Lord, revive thy work in the midst of the years, in the midst of the years make known; in wrath remember mercy. (Habakkuk 3:2)

CHAPTER THIRTY-SEVEN:

1. Zephaniah.

2. To warn Israel and all nations of the judgment of God.

3. Israel.

4. God is mighty to save.

5. The Lord thy God in the midst of thee is mighty; He will save, He will rejoice over thee with joy; He will rest in his love, He will joy over thee with singing. (Zephaniah 3:17)

CHAPTER THIRTY-EIGHT:

1. Haggai.

2. To inspire Israel to new zeal for God and make the leaders aware of their responsibility to rebuild the temple of worship.

3. Israel.

4. Building God's Kingdom should be a priority of the true believer.

5. Now therefore thus saith the Lord of hosts; Consider your ways. (Haggai 1:5)

CHAPTER THIRTY-NINE:

1. Zechariah.

2. To inspire Israel to finish the temple.

3. Israel.

4. God controls the affairs of men and nations.

5. In that day there shall be a fountain opened to the house of David and to the inhabitants of Jerusalem for sin and for uncleanness. (Zechariah 13:1)

CHAPTER FORTY:

1. Malachi.

2. To call the nation of Israel to repentance and return to righteousness.

3. Israel.

4. Repentance and returning equal restoration. Both attitude and action are necessary for forgiveness.

5. If ye will not hear, and if ye will not lay it to heart, to give glory unto my name, saith the Lord of hosts, I will even send a curse upon you, and I will curse your blessings: yea, I have cursed them already, because ye do not lay it to heart. (Malachi 2:2)

CPSIA information can be obtained
at www.ICGtesting.com
Printed in the USA
FSOW03n0633150317
31737FS